ABOUT NOBODY SPECIAL

Essays on an American Life

ABOUT NOBODY SPECIAL

Essays on an American Life

By

John Barry

OTHER BOOKS BY JOHN BARRY

THE ZOMBIE GARDENER, BOOK 1
THE ZOMBIE GARDENER, BOOK 2

Table of Contents

This one is for Dad;
Thank you for introducing me to my dreams.
Thank you for teaching me about life, about love and everything in between.
Thank you for being Dad first, no matter how hard or hurtful it may have been.
Thank you for our short time together,
making me somebody special.

THANK YOU

The one thing I learned about the writing life is unless you do it every day, and make decent money, it's really not a thing to most people. It's like playing drums in a band that has a steady weekend gig; unless you have a number of albums and are playing in what ever the Boston Garden is being called these days, it really is just a little better than a hobby.

At least in the eyes of most people.

I am lucky in that I have had people in my life that have openly supported my writing, even when it really was just better than a hobby:

Bobby Sheehan, who even back when I was a long-haired angry teenager would open every conversation with 'what have you written lately.'

My friend Paul, who openly looked forward to and enjoyed my long letters about nothing. I will miss writing them. Rest in peace my friend.

My brother Buddy, who may not fully understand my life and the decisions I make, who has never had to say but has always let it be known he is just a phone call away.

Thank You

I want to also thank my editor Kristy, who during her own life changing events found the time to ask the right questions, suggest the right solutions and do the hard job of telling me "It doesn't make sense, you may want to change this."

Of course, the biggest thank you goes out to my family and the staff of Edible Arrangements Foxboro for the many times you were the perfect 'captive audience'. Thank you for your patience and keeping the eye rolls to a minimum.

Finally, I would like to thank my biggest fan, actually I think he's my only fan, Mike Barry. Your excitement over my writing is infectious, encouraging and welcomed. Just as long as you continue to follow the terms of the restraining order.

A SHARED MEMORY

A shared memory.
Like fog rolling across the horizon,
Tendrils of misty sights and smells,
Of a day long past.
We each lived within those same moments.
Each experienced a life under the same roof.
Except, memories from different eyes
Often have differing emotions;
Hardship and want,
Become an awkward discomfort.
Hurt and deceit,
Become a dishonest misunderstanding.
Green becomes blue.
A shared memory
Is but a difference of opinion,
And this opinion is through my eyes.

I AM ME

I'm an asshole.

A stubborn bastard.

I am blunt, to the point, and rough of opinion.

I don't know why I'm like this; it's not like I try to be an asshole. I don't wake up every morning thinking of new asshole stuff to do, and to be honest most times I don't even realize I'm being an asshole. It just seems to happen. One moment I have everyone laughing and happy to be in my presence, and in the next, my wife is shaking her head and we're being de-friended off of social media pages.

I've learned a long time ago to make no excuses for it, and have accepted the fact that this is who I am.

My mother once told me, "Dealing with you is like chewing on broken glass."

It sounds harsh, but my mother said a lot of mean things to all of her children. Yet, I'm not so sure she was far off with this one. I am fully aware that when I'm having one of my moments, I can be brutally stubborn and borderline mean.

Yet, I am just me: nobody special.

An asshole, yes, but do the events of my life warrant a book to figure out why? Because that was the ultimate goal here; to figure out why I am the way I am. What makes me think the way I do, say the things I do, and act the way I do.

Basically, why am I an asshole.

On the plus side, I have tried to not make this a chronicle of someone unimportant; instead, I've tried to make this a collection of stories you may find interesting, or at the very least find enjoyable for the moment.

For my family, I say each of us have lived through most of what I write here. We all experienced it under the same roof. Please understand these events are through my eyes and may differ somewhat from what you remember. It is not unlike four people at an intersection witnessing a car accident and then give four differing accounts. The same goes with these shared memories.

The details may differ, but the events are true.

MAY 8, 1976

A punch will only hurt for a little while, but your pride will hurt forever.
                                              --The wisdom of Dad

A SIMPLE BREATH

A simple breath,
Unforced,
Passing through still warm-parted lips.
It swirls around the room
Gently caressing flushed, tear-stained cheeks.
Continually floating upwards
To assimilate with the breaths of a thousand more.
A simple breath
Whispering goodbye.

GROUND ZERO

I Hate You!

The ghostly whisper, coming from nowhere and everywhere all at once, repeating those three words, slowly pulling me up from the depths of sleep.

I Hate You!

It felt like gray misty fingers gripped my brain, trying to keep me in that sleep-wake world where dreams become real and reality becomes a dream. It seemed like I was looking up from the bottom of a pool; I see an opening, a murky wavy light, and I reach up.

I Hate You!

The words begin to distort, to change into something at first unrecognizable, with each second becoming more a noise and less a voice. I reach the dream opening, and the words change into a slow, scuffling footstep. Not from my dream world, but coming up the stairs outside my room.

My sleep-crusted brain was pushing hard to jump-start, sluggish from too much sleep. I couldn't focus on what seemed to be a lot of commotion going on. Something was happening outside my window; there seemed to be a fair amount of voices coming from downstairs, far too many doors opening and closing, and the footsteps, slow and steady, I could tell were now coming down the hallway.

I restarted to the nearest focus point: yesterday, skipping school, Dad yelling, me yelling.

"I got a call from the school," Dad in that deep, slow way that is still the voice in my head. "They said you weren't in today."

I had a long speech ready; missing buses, sudden illnesses, and even the constitutional rights of the American student to take a day off now and then, but all I did was stand there, my mouth open and sleep drool drying on my cheek.

"Nothing?!" His voice was getting louder. "I had to deal with this shit with your brothers, and I'm not doing this with you!"

His voice now at wall -shaking decibels, his large weather-worn hand outstretched and shaking with the index finger pointed at me. Again, my voice

7

was lost, hiding somewhere in my gut that was now twisted and ready to spew up anything in it.

"Still nothing to say?!" His face looked down at me in true anger, and something else, something showing in the crow's feet behind his glasses.

It took me years to understand what that look was: it was the look of disappointment.

"You can think about it all weekend, then." His voice took a sudden drop to just above a whisper, a sad whisper in my memory. "I'm going to Uncle John's for the night, we'll talk tomorrow." And he turned and began walking down the stairs.

The biggest mystery of my life is why I did what happened next. I had stood there, quiet for all that time, not knowing what to say, not wanting to say anything. So, why did I choose when he was walking down the stairs to finally speak my mind?

"I fucking hate you!" I yelled, and slammed the door shut.

I stood frozen in place, wide-eyed, horrified and unable to move my gaze away from the back of the door. I was certain the next thing would be his work boots storming back up the stairs, the door slamming open, and a large calloused hand slapping the back of my head. Instead, it was quiet, then Dad's footsteps continued down the stairs. They sounded heavier, slower.

It was such a cowardly thing for me to do.

The sleep fog dissipated, bringing me fully back to the real world.

The footsteps reached my bedroom door and paused a moment. I was sure it was Dad ready to pick up the argument where it ended yesterday. I could almost hear the years of tarnish grinding as the knob turned. The door gave a sudden creak as if a hand on the other side was placed on it, ready to push. Then the door opened. Hard.

It wasn't Dad. I recognized the short, rounded silhouette immediately as mom dressed in her old flowery robe. She took a step into the room, her brown and gray hair slightly wild with strands flying free from the dozens of bobby-pins she always seemed to have in there. Her face already showed the deep, permanent creases that gave her that constant look of anger.

"Get your fat ass out of bed," she said, slow and without emotion. "Your father died."

Then she turned and walked out.

What the hell did she just say?

All of a sudden, my 14 year old brain kick-started and everything slammed into focus at once.

The front door opened and closed as if someone was doing it on purpose, but I could tell by the muffled voices it was people coming in and going out.

There was a deep, pain-filled howl that at first I couldn't identify, but it was followed by a long, soul-wrenching, "Noooo!". My Aunt's voice, my father's sister. I could tell as the loud deep sobs faded that someone must have brought her inside.

Your father died.

She did say that, right?

I know, I know. She also said, "Get your fat ass out of bed." Most moms called their sons 'Little Man', or 'my Little Buddy'; my mom called me 'fat ass'. So, what? At some point, I stopped hearing it.

But, she did say my father died. People coming and going. People screaming. People crying. It all connected.

My father died!

Then the voice in my head came alive; last night I told him I hated him.

No, you told him, "I fucking hate you!"

I'm not sure how long I laid in bed after my mother left the room. I was horrified, confused, and scared to the point I couldn't move. It was like my brain wouldn't grasp the main event and was stuck on all these little details; I'd never experienced death, never had anyone close to me die. I had no idea what I was supposed to do now. I wasn't even sure if I was supposed to be crying, because I didn't feel like crying.

I felt like screaming.

I thought someone eventually would come up and talk to me at least. Someone needed to hug me until I cried and keep hugging me until my eyes had nothing more to give. Someone with my face held gently in their hands explaining to me what was going to happen over the next couple days, and months, and years. I knew there was no one in my life like that, but I hoped.

"Tommy's home," an unknown voice said from downstairs.

One of my brothers. He was in the Air Force and had been given emergency leave to come home. It was enough to get me out of bed and jogging down the stairs. I was halfway through the kitchen when Mom grabbed my arm and twisted me around to face her. The room, which was filled with voices of her friends, instantly became silent and all heads turned in my direction.

"I'm about to come into some money," Mom sneered. Yes, she actually sneered. "So, you better play your cards right."

I had no idea what the hell that meant, no idea at all. You get money when someone dies? Is there a card game or something at the funeral? What the fuck was she talking about?

She squeezed my arm tighter, and pain began shooting out where her fingers dug into my skin. Her eyes squinted, staring me down, lips clenched so they were nothing more than a thin line. She held on for a moment, then two, then three, and then let go.

I backed away slowly at first, unconsciously rubbing the spot on my arm that still had the impression of her fingers, then when I was sure it was safe I turned and bolted out the back door.

IV

It seemed like time over the next three days warped in and out of reality. There are blocks of time still gone today, still out of reach. It's like the gatekeeper in my brain has them locked away in some deep, dark dungeon and refuses to release them to the surface.

Then there are these quirky little snippets that have been skipping around my skull for decades. Always dancing in the background, but always ready to jump to the front when called.

A weird little family lived across the front walkway from us. The father, always dressed in the same food-stained shirt and oversized work pants, smelled to high heaven of body odor and talked as if he had a mouth full of rocks. It was like the words got jumbled around before coming out into the open air. The mother seemed to always stand in the doorway and smile at you as you passed by; I'm not talking sweet old lady smile-- this was more of the creepy, open-mouthed, toothless grin that raised the hairs on your neck smile. The daughter who was in her twenties, but mentally in her pre-teens, was pregnant. The talk amongst the grownups had the father as both granddad and dad to his daughter's baby.

At some point that weekend, this smelly old man came across the walkway offering his condolences to my mother, then asking her to bake him an apple pie. I shit you not. Funeral arrangements hadn't even been finalized, and this guy was asking my mother to bake him a pie.

My brother Buddy caught wind of this and I can still see him stomping off, slamming open the front door, and yelling across the walkway, "Stay away from my mother, and make your own damn pie!" He slammed the door closed, hard enough that I bet the window panes are still rattling.

Somehow, my brother-in-law Paul got the short straw and had to identify my father's body. I didn't know this until years later, and I didn't know how hard that was on him. When he came back to the house, he gave my mother the bag of my father's belongings, and of course she immediately removed anything of value. For some odd and grotesque reason, my mother pulled out a silver object, gave it a quick look over, and handed it to me. It was my father's watch: the old silver Timex he wore all the time and was wearing that day.

I was still having a hard time grasping what was going on, still trying to understand what 'your father died' actually meant. Up till then, none of it seemed real to me, but as I looked down at the broken watch in my hands, it became very real, very fast.

The glass had a number of cracks spider-webbing across the face. A tiny, pyramid-sized piece of glass where two cracks intersected had popped out, leaving a hole the size of a pencil eraser in the top corner. Either from blunt force or exposure, the watch had stopped, the hands frozen at 2:12 and the date at May 8. What made it even more real was the silver expandable wrist band was still splattered in my father's blood.

I kept that watch until I moved out of my mother's house; I never fixed it, and the blood eventually wore off with time. I think today I can say the watch wasn't so much a reminder of Dad, but a reminder to me of how angry I was that he died in the way he did, when he did. For many years, I was angry at the other two men in the car who survived, I was angry at my mother for being so casual about it all, and mostly, I was angry at God for taking my father when I needed him the most.

I also never connected the watch to my mother. All those years I was consumed by hate that I never asked the one basic question: why would a mother hand her young son his father's watch, still covered in blood, on the day he learns of his father's death? Why did she do that? What reaction was she hoping for?

Was it ignorance brought on by grief, or something a bit more sinister?

When I decided it was time to move out, I figured I needed to leave the anger behind as well. I left the watch behind in a box with some other stuff, and a few weeks later discovered my mother had thrown the box out.

I remember my first day back to school. In shop class, a kid came up and asked where I'd been. I was sitting on a workbench in woodshop, my feet swinging, and I looked down to the sawdust-covered floor before I answered. I didn't say anything for a moment; I even thought of not saying anything at all, but for some weird reason I smiled.

"My father died," I said, through the grin.

"Why you smiling?" He had a look of disgust on his face, and I could tell he was horrified, and he turned and walked away. I never before, and have never since, experienced a 'grief' smile like that.

It took a good ten minutes for the smile to slowly fade.

I ended up riding in my sister Mary Ellen's car at one point during that weekend. I was in the back, and my sister was about to pull into a spot in the common parking area in front of our apartment, when there was a bang and I was flung into the back of her seat. As I sat up, I saw she was crying uncontrollably, her hands frozen on the steering wheel. I'm not sure whose car she ran into, I believe it was my brother Buddy's, but as a crowd of brothers and cousins came to her rescue, she kept repeating that as she was turning, she saw someone going into the house and she thought it was Dad.

I never told her, until this moment, that I saw the same thing.

I also thought it was Dad.

GOD IS NOT MY FRIEND ANYMORE

TERMINAL HATE

My father died.
It was a car accident that took him.
I wasn't driving. I wasn't in the car.
He wasn't going to or from anything that involved me.
I didn't cause it, had nothing to do with it,
Nothing I could have done to change it.
But, I told him I hated him.
They were the last words a man heard from his 14-year-old son.
Three simple words that trapped me,
Like prison bars of a condemned soul facing an eternal sentence.
My father's booming voice repeating them in my dreams,
And whispering at me through the wind in the trees.
Just three words, bouncing around my head at a deafening roar,
Until it was all I could hear.

FATE

Over the course of a few days, I was able to get a patch-work version of what the hell happened to my father.

Dad was a member of a local men's social club here in Brockton, Massachusetts called 'The Fraternal Order of Eagles'. Back in Brockton's glory days, when it was the leader in shoe manufacturing in the country, factory workers established what was nothing more than private drinking establishments. Over the decades, they became more community-based with fundraising for local charities, but they are still first and foremost a safe place for members to drink and socialize.

From what I understand, the Brockton chapter was a breath away from closing its doors and dissolving its charter. My father's goal was to restructure, rebuild, and turn it back into a club in good standing. It became his pet project.

My Uncle John, Dad's brother, was on the board of the same fraternity, but his club was somewhere in or around the town of Sturbridge, Massachusetts. Uncle John's club had faced the same slow death as the Brockton club, but he and his members were able to breathe new life into it. Dad wanted to know what this other club did and maybe do the same in Brockton, so Uncle John set up a meeting with the club's officers.

Since my father didn't drive, he never had a license, he convinced his best friend Jack and another friend Bill to drive him; they were both members of the Brockton club as well.

The plan was for them to go to Uncle John's club out in Sturbridge, then spend Friday night after the meeting at my Uncle's place, and come home early Saturday morning. I'm sure there were a few beers consumed before, during, and after, so it would have been a wise decision for them to sleep over. That is, until a girlfriend got involved.

Both Jack and Bill were dating moms from our street, and one of them was not happy at all about the boys going on this road trip. There were words exchanged, probably some raised voices, and at least one threat of, *If you don't come home*

15

tonight, don't come home at all-- words that set in motion the disaster that changed my world.

The scene is set: three men who had already put in eight hours of work set off on a two-hour drive across the state. They spend the next five hours or more at a Fraternal Order of Eagles social club for a meet-and-greet where alcohol is readily being served. Sometime after midnight, the three men, already up for over 18 hours and under the influence, head out on a return two-hour late-night drive home.

Bill is driving; Jack is in the back; Dad is riding shotgun.

At some point, Jack stretches out on the back seat and falls asleep.

We can only assume Dad soon dozes off as well.

Bill loses his battle with consciousness and falls asleep at the wheel.

The car is now speeding down a nearly empty highway with no one in control.

It drifts off the highway onto the shoulder, and then into a ditch.

The ditch forces the car into a roll, which ejects the still-sleeping Jack.

Jack's body smashes through the back window and lands somewhere in the ditch.

Both Bill and Dad remain trapped as the car rolls over.

Dad is crushed as the ground collapses the roof above his head.

Bill and Jack receive injuries requiring hospitalization, but soon recover.

Dad is pronounced dead at the scene.

I don't remember seeing either Jack or Bill at the wake or funeral. Either they were still in the hospital recovering, or I was so overwhelmed that I didn't notice them.

For a long time, my hate for the two of them was only equal to the hate I had towards the moms who demanded they drive home that night. Jack received the bulk of it: he was my Dad's best friend, and had even lived with us for a while. He should have protected my father better.

It was years before I understood that I really didn't hate them. I was mad, yes, but I didn't blame them. Not fully, anyways.

The accident was nobody's and everybody's fault all at the same time. I guess I was mad because they survived.

AN IRISH WAKE

We were going to a wake.

My father's wake.

Whatever the hell that means.

I was a 14-year-old kid from the projects who'd never had anyone close to me die. I had never been to a funeral home, had never attended a funeral. All I knew at the time was that I had to get dressed up and pay respects to Dad. I really had no idea what that meant. No clue what I was supposed to do, what to expect, and what the fuck a "wake" was anyway.

My brothers and sister were in as deep a shock as I. Dad was the glue, the roots of our family tree, and without the roots, the branches were scrambling around trying to figure out what to do next. My younger brother Billy and I got lost in the emotional dust cloud that was swirling above all our heads. Somebody did come up with the idea that Billy was too young to attend either the wake or funeral, and it's a debate that continues today.

Billy was only 8, but today he will tell you that instead of being shipped off to a babysitter, he wished he was part of it. Even if it left him with some emotional scars, it would be better than not feeling anything at all.

Billy once confided in me no one actually told him Dad had died. He said he knew something bad was up because of all the people coming and going. He felt invisible, overwhelmed, and went and hid behind the bushes outside the living room window. He was there for hours playing in the dirt with some toy trucks; no one noticed he was gone.

The window above him was open and he told me he could hear all the conversations: some muffled, some jumbled, and most in bits and pieces intermixing like someone changing the channels on the radio really fast.

He was able to grasp enough to understand he no longer had a father.

So, he continued to play in the dirt until he got hungry.

Neither my father nor mother had a license to drive. I heard stories over the years that included Dad refused to drive as long as he was drinking, and that when he was younger he got into an accident of some sort that convinced him to never

17

drive again. I'm sure there is some truth to all of the stories, but all that matters is that he didn't drive and had never owned a vehicle during my lifetime. I'm pretty sure Mom couldn't drive because of her battle with epilepsy.

Because of this, growing up there were no vacation road trips, no Sunday drives, no trips to parks, and I was 18 before I experienced a meal inside an actual restaurant-- at least, a restaurant where the server wasn't wearing a paper hat. My world was land-locked, and it consisted of the street I lived on, the school I attended, and the occasional sleepover at my sister Mary Ellen's or brother Buddy's apartments.

It was a rare event that I got a chance to go for a ride anywhere in a car, and the trip to the funeral home was no exception. The ride created enough of an excitement buzz in me that when we arrived, I bolted out of the car with a smile. For a brief moment the weekend from hell was set aside and I was enjoying the excitement of just being someplace else, ignorant of what was about to unfold, and oblivious to what lay within the pretty white building before me.

I saw Tommy entering a side door.

"Tommy!" I yelled, my smile growing wider.

He didn't hear me and continued in.

I bolted after him, forgetting the real reason I was there.

I ran up the stairs and threw open the door. The sudden change from bright sun to the dark hallway inside briefly blinded me, and I stood for a moment to let my eyes adjust.

I could hear voices just ahead, some crying, and the excitement quickly drained as I remembered this had to do with the death of my father.

I wanted my brothers, my sister, any of them, all of them. My eyes adjusted and I continued down the small hallway. The walls were covered in a dark oak paneling that seemed to absorb any light, and they gave off a smell of strong cleanser and oil that made me feel a little light-headed. There was another smell floating above my head, like the scent of a thousand flowers all mixed together. It should have been pleasant and comforting, but intertwined within it was something else, something old and off-putting that made me not want to go any further.

I could now hear my sister talking and it was enough to return some strength to my legs.

Still unnerved by the hallway, I turned the corner into a larger, brighter room full of wooden folding chairs lined up in neat little rows. Along each wall, baskets of flowers, more than I've ever seen at once, were lined in almost a V-shape. Its colorful array tunneled my vision to the front of the room.

There it was. A casket. The bottom half was draped in even more flowers; the top lid was sitting open, exposing a man lying inside. A man whom just days before I told to his face I hated.

He didn't look real, lying there in a suit, his skin yellowish and looking almost plastic. I had seen him asleep a thousand times: on the couch with a leg and an arm hanging down to the floor; in his chair with head tilted down and a non-filtered Pall-Mall cigarette still slowly burning between his fingers; and even sitting at the kitchen table with his crossed arms used as a pillow. What I saw before me-- eyes closed, head tilted so the chin looked forced into the bulky chest-- was not my father. Could not be my father. Should not be my father.

Voices behind me broke my trance, and when I shot a look back, I saw a room off to the side with the same wooden chairs lined up in the same neat little rows. Without a word, without thought I rushed to the side room, finding the furthest chair out of view and dropping into it.

I was in shock, a breath away from losing it, and in dire need of a friendly voice, a simple explanation, a hug.

Like my brother Billy behind the bushes, I felt invisible.

That chair became my world. The wall that now separated me from my father's casket became my protector.

In that chair, sitting on my hands and rocking back and forth, it felt like all at once my nerve endings came alive. I could even feel the adrenaline burning in my veins, racing to explode out of my fingertips. The emotions were so intense that even 40 years later, my brain is careful what it lets drip out into my consciousness.

On the other side of that wall is a casket, and inside that casket is my father, my Dad, and the last time he heard my voice I told him I hated him.

Again, you didn't tell him you hated him, you told him you 'fucking hated him', and let's toss a couple exclamation points at the end of that.

It was all I could handle, and I was thankful for my brain's ability to be a human circuit breaker and sense my emotional pain was in the red. I went into partial shutdown for the next two days, which is why I have such hodge-podge images. I was aware there were a lot of people because Dad was a popular guy, but their images are a distorted blur, like a hundred ghost milling around.

Maybe they were ghost.

Some of the people found me rocking in my chair in the side room. Most felt the need to approach me and all had stupid things to say. I was good, I politely shook their hands, smiled and nodded. Inside though, I had plenty to say to them.

"He's in a better place now."

A better place? Really? Are you saying it's worse here with us?

"At least he's not feeling any pain."

How about I kick you in the balls and see how much pain you'll feel?

"You're the man of the house now."

I'm only 14, you ass.

"He's with God now."

Fuck you!

Because of her 'play your cards right' statement, I had avoided my mother as much as possible. Except for the handful of people who ventured in, I pretty much had the room to myself. I was invisible, but then again, not so much.

Maybe the few people coming in to give me their condolences caught her eye, but Mom finally saw me. There were no hugs, no back rubs, no asking if I was OK because it had to have been obvious I was far from OK. I don't remember any talk from her at all.

There was a hand on my arm pulling me out of the chair, and not unlike the nuns marching you to the principal's office, she began walking me towards, then around, my protective wall. I began to resist, but a firm squeeze on my upper arm convinced me to keep moving. All I could do was keep my head down and my eyes on the floor.

I didn't want to see him. I didn't want to see my Dad like that. I was terrified and my body was shaking from its core. Mom either didn't notice or didn't care.

When we arrived in front of the casket she released my arm, then she walked away.

GOD IS NOT MY FRIEND ANYMORE

The boy kneeled in front of the casket
On the stool with the faded red pad.
He had never experienced death,
Had never seen a dead body up close,
So, he kept his eyes pointed downward towards the floor.
Thinking if he made believe he was in church it will be ok,
But it was not ok, Church was not ok,
In church was God, and God was not his friend anymore.
A single tear slowly rolled down his cheek,
And blindly he reached into the casket.
His fingers touching something cold, something unreal.
He glanced up seeing large entwined weather-worn hands,
Hands he recognized,
And the single tear was followed by many more.
His breath hitched,
Uncontrollable sobs coming so fast,
Faster than his breath,
Until both became stuck,
And his chest felt ready to explode.
He opened his mouth to scream
But neither voice nor air came out.
From behind someone grabbed him, his sister,
And he wanted to tell her he couldn't breathe, couldn't scream
But realized he had been screaming all along.
As she walked him out of the room he looked back, one last look.
Goodbye, Dad.

I was now completely broken. My brain shut down, shoving everything else from that point on into a locked room in my head. Even today I am left with random images playing *Whac-A-Mole* with my consciousness.

I can remember for some reason being overly excited by the automatic windows. It was my first time in a limousine, and for the entire twenty-minute trip from the house to the church I had my finger on that window button. I was just amazed as the window slowly went down, then slowly back up again, then slowly down and over and over and over again.

Nobody told me to stop.

Another *Whac-A-Mole* moment is the only clear memory I have of the cemetery service itself. As expected, my siblings and I were lined up in front of the casket with me at the end. My vantage point was the edge of the casket and the frame of the stand that lowers it into the ground. Most of the frame was covered by something that was supposed to mimic green grass, but failed and looked like what it was: a rug of unnatural bright green plastic grass-like strips.

At some point someone either kicked or the wind blew the corner flap of that green shit over, exposing the hole beneath. Of course, the best vantage point for this was where I was standing. I could hear nothing else, I could see nothing else; all I could do was focus on that hole under the casket.

What finally woke me from the trance were the gunshots. Dad was a veteran and the local VFW sent over an Honor Guard. My body jumped with each loud crack from the rifle, and the gun smoke seem to roll across the field in front of us as the bagpipes started "Amazing Grace." That's all it took to begin another breakdown, and once again the sobs came faster than my breath, and once again hands were laid on my shoulder to help calm me down.

I looked up expecting to see my sister, but was shocked to see the tear-distorted face of my Dad looking down at me. I blinked to clear my eyes and realized it was Uncle John.

"Amazing Grace" was over, the service ended and I came to grips with the fact Dad was really gone.

DELIVER ME

For most of my adult life I would take one day each week and have lunch with Dad. I would sit at the gravesite and hold long, out loud, conversations with him. I would debate current events and ask serious questions on my life, and try to decipher the 'caws' from the crows for the answer.

I found comfort in it.

My wife grew concerned over this, and one day asked if I should go and speak with someone.

"When my Dad starts talking back to me, then I'll go see someone." I told her.

DAD

I can still feel your rough, weather-worn hands,
That taught me the rewards of hard work.

I can still see the deep, tired look on your face,
That taught me the meaning of providing for your family.

I can still sense your large arm around my shoulders,
That taught me how to feel safe during the storms of the night.

I can still hear your booming voice,
So many words that taught me so many things.

The many years may have eased the pain of your passing,
But have not diminished the strength of your spirit.

Inspired from my favorite picture of Dad:

Your roaring voice yelling "Deliver Me!" as your arms stretched out and upwards. Your round bearded face exploding in smile, eyes half closed in a deep, crows' feet squint, twinkling and looking to the heavens.

LIFE OF DAD

He was born July 16, 1926, the second of four children, and died just two months shy of his fiftieth birthday. He was the first of his generation to leave us. Today, in my world, you could say he died a young man, and he did. Although, I try to think that he lived to pass cigars around for the birth of six children and was alive to hold three of his eighteen grandchildren. He walked his only daughter down the aisle and stood witness as his oldest son said his wedding vows. He raised four of his six children to adulthood, two of whom honorably served their country. He also survived three wars, one of which he participated in.

The mark of time ran quickly for him, challenging him at every step. Life was not so good for this hardworking man, but he was still able to leave his mark on all of us.

SHE WAS MY GRANDMOTHER

Her name was Pauline Eis.

On August 25, 1924 in a small ceremony in Mamaroneck, New York, she married Fredrick Harold Barry, my Grandfather. Pauline was 21 years old on that day, and using simple math was also very pregnant with my Uncle Bill. There is not much out there on how the two met, how long they dated, or any of the details of what seemed to be an old-fashioned shotgun-type wedding. The Eis side of the family is all but unknown to any of us, and as far as I know, neither side has ever had any contact with each other.

My Grandmother's parents, Anton and Leopoline Eis, both emigrated here from Bohemia, what is now Czechoslovakia, and it is a safe bet that on that warm summer afternoon they didn't understand the path their daughter chose. They didn't realize their own travels over land and ocean to a better life may have influenced their daughter to travel over 200 miles to her own terrifying, but exciting future.

My Grandmother left her parents and her family to be with my Grandfather, and there are no records to show if Anton, Leopoline, or daughter Pauline ever saw or communicated with each other ever again.

All things point to my Grandfather not being too much to think about; he is listed as being a rubber worker, but a number of the census polls listed him as unemployed. Town reports not only list numerous noise complaints at their house, but also shows my Grandfather with an extensive police record for public intoxication.

My mother told me a story of my Grandfather arriving to my Grandmother's funeral in handcuffs, having been arrested the night before. I have never been able to prove or disprove this story, my mother not remembering who she heard it from, and by the time I learned of it, my Aunt and Uncles were all gone. I also have no recollection of ever meeting my Grandfather; he spent his last years in a VA hospital bed, suffering from alcohol-related ailments. He died two years prior to my father.

My Grandfather had no property, no apartment, no prospects for a new family, and moved my Grandmother into his parents' house which still stands today. It is a small salt-box of a house I can only describe as the size of a garage with a second floor. The house was already filled with my Great-Grandparents and a Great-Aunt, and seven months later my Uncle Bill was born, adding another wrinkle to my Grandmother's already cramped life. It was there, in Stoughton, Massachusetts-- what was then a poor working-class community-- that Pauline began to realize the bleak future that awaited her.

In the span of three years my Grandmother gave birth to three more children; my Dad in 1926, my Uncle John in 1927, and my Aunt Evelyn in 1928. Sadly, their growing family didn't seem to motivate my Grandfather, and when Pauline got pregnant again, feeling alone and trapped in a tiny house with over nine people inside, she just couldn't bring herself to birth another child.

It was the winter of 1931, and under a fog of emotional stress and the fear of religious damnation, she made her choice. Against the criminal laws of the time, and the religious laws of a strict Irish Catholic family, she decided to have an abortion.

In the 1930s there were no walk-in clinics, no office visits with bright, clean exam rooms, or safe and sterile procedures. In most cases 'kitchen table surgery' was performed, where literally a table was set up in any available space, including the patient's living room. There were no pain medications, no sedatives, and no antibiotics. What would be an uncomfortable ten minutes today, in 1931 would be a long and very painful ordeal.

There are no records of where or how it took place, only the end result.

My Grandmother's abortion led to a blood infection-- septicemia-- and she died on her 28th birthday.

My father was just five years old.

Today, there are no known family photographs or hand-written letters to show she ever existed. Her own children knew of her, but never knew her. They had no memory of her face, and no stories of her life to pass down. Her grandchildren grew up without ever knowing her name. The only things that show she lived and died is a gravestone she shares with other family members, and a certificate listing her cause of death.

Her name was Pauline Eis, and she was my Grandmother.

THE MAKING OF A TOUGH GUY

In his pre-teen years Dad came down with a virus that caused the loss of all the hair on his body. It doesn't matter where you live-- big city or a small country town-- you show up to school bald-headed with no eyebrows and you're facing the brunt of bullies, gangs, and classmates. I can't even imagine the hell it must have been for him to walk into school each day.

It's human nature when faced with this kind of aggression to either build up emotional barriers and hide within yourself, or stand up and fight your way through it. Fight or flight, it's called, and Dad chose to fight-- and he got good at it. He ended up with a reputation of being a *tough guy*, a title he didn't want and wasn't proud of, but it was also the main reason he always sided with the underdog and came to the rescue of those being bullied.

The fighting lasted through middle school and into high school, and eventually got to be too much for him so he made what became one of his biggest regrets: he quit school. This regret became the driving force behind him pushing all of us to go as far as we could with education, and no doubt the reason he was so angry the day I skipped.

He may have felt he had no choice but to quit school, but he knew he had a choice to not be like his father: drunk, broke, and an outcast. At 17 he joined the Navy, bald, but eager for a new challenge.

By all reports the Navy did change him for the better and when his tour was done he had a chest full of medals, a commendation from the president, memories of a very exotic girlfriend, and a full head of hair. No shit, after all those years, all those doctors scratching their own heads, it took a tour in the Navy and a world war to bring his hair back. A mystery to all but Dad; he was convinced it was the salt water that did it.

In my life each September he would stop shaving until the following spring. By Christmas, he would have a full beard touching his chest. One picture shows Dad in the kitchen doorway, arms spread out, and a smiling bearded face. Even today I can see him that way, lifting his head to the ceiling, and yelling in his deep voice, "Deliver me!"

"Bob, why do you grow a beard each winter?"

"Because I can."

It was almost as if his hair was making up for lost time and was now growing wild. Except on his legs, which till the day he died were as bald and smooth as a baby's ass.

Picture this: a man, six-foot-something, broad-shouldered, skin dark from years of working shirtless in the summer sun, steps out of a rented cottage at the beach. It is one of the few times he wears shorts and his glowing, white, hairless legs are a shocking contrast to his tanned torso.

Every summer my aunt would rent a cottage at Swifts Beach for a couple weeks, and at least one weekend we would all be invited down. It was the only chance to see Dad in shorts and yes, his legs were blinding white and totally hairless.

He took advantage of the opportunity and would walk into the water up to his waist, and stand there for hours, convinced the salt water would work again and bring hair back to his legs.

It might seem silly, but to him it was an important goal, a goal worth working for no matter how many odds were against him.

SUPER-SECRET PHOTO ALBUM

I think I was ten when I discovered Dad's super-secret photo album, and I'm not sure but I think it was my brother Tom who hinted at its existence. If so, I am eternally grateful to him.

The album was tucked deep in the darkest corner of his dresser bottom drawer, hidden under a camouflage of random clothes nobody would ever care to look under. In my memory, the album was dark brown, and had no markings on the outside. It was as long as a magazine, but wider, like a legal-sized paper turned on its side. The pages inside were cardboard, yellowed with age and with a sticky coating that held the photos in place. Sandwiched over the pages was a clear plastic sheet that covered the photos, but you could pull it aside if you wanted to take the photos out. My brain tells me there were no more than twelve cardboard pages in all.

Inside were photos of just one girl.

I could tell her skin was golden brown, even though the photos were all black and white. At least that's what I imagined, and I also imagined her straight, waist length hair was a jet black that captured the reflection of the sun. Her oval face and high cheekbones framed what I knew must have been chestnut brown eyes that were both sleepy and inviting. In all the photos she also had a touch of that smile, relaxed and contented, as if she just woke up and was happy with the world.

Did I also mention she was dressed in what I believe was a real grass skirt, and nothing else?

Unlike the big boobs of the models in the magazines, her breasts were small, perky, and for some reason more exciting. In some of the pictures her leg creeps out of the skirt, exposing it up to her thigh. It is those shots that really got my heart pounding and my head spinning.

This, my friends, based on what I have been told, is the girlfriend my Dad had when he was stationed in Hawaii during the war.

I'd already discovered Dad's girly magazines a few years prior. They were in his dresser top drawer, half-ass hidden under socks and underwear. They were OK, they served a purpose, and every couple of months he rotated the stock with new stuff. Like any all-American, puberty-blinded young man, a picture of a naked girl is a picture of a naked girl. Yet, even then, I knew those girls were not totally real-- they were models made up to look that way-- but a photo of a native Hawaiian girl was as close to real as a ten-year-old boy could handle.

I don't know where that photo album went. Not long after Dad died it disappeared, either to one of my siblings, or Mom tossed it in the trash with no regard to its historic value to the family.

I often wondered when my Mom was at her worst if Dad pulled out that album and dreamed *what if*.

THE CONTRADICTION OF DAD

I was young, still in the lower half of single digits, and by the time I got to the crowd they were already two-deep. I was able to squeeze through the maze of legs and got close enough to see Dad straddled on top of some guy. Seeing my Dad in a street fight was shocking enough, but seeing him in a blind rage scared the living shit out of me. His face was contorted in anger, and those hammer-like arms were coming down fast and hard on the poor bastard's upper body and head.

Years later I was told this was a police officer who was assigned to walk the street. The guy had either pushed my sister off a bench or confronted her and her boyfriend, telling them he didn't want 'trash' on public property. Either way, my father witnessed it and pounced onto the poor bastard.

This was just one event of many that locked in the legend that was Dad. He was the local tough guy, the don't-mess-with-my-family guy, and the loyal friend to a fault guy. Years after Dad died, I met my future wife's family for the first time. Her stepfather was the nephew of one of my father's friends, a man whispered to be 'connected'. Her stepfather pulled her aside and told her my father was a well-known leg-breaker for his Uncle.

Another mystery we will never solve.

By the time my screaming ass came out into the world, Dad was fast on his way to mellowing out. Most of the legends that surrounded Dad came to me in stories, and one that made an impression on me involved the convenience store owned by a man known to not like anyone from the projects.

It was a hot day and Dad gave my sister a couple dollars and had her go to the store and buy us hood-rats some popsicles. The store goes that my sister placed a dozen or so popsicles on the counter and asked the owner for a bag. Once again, my sister was called Hill Street Trash and she rushed home crying with the melting popsicles cradled in her arms.

Eventually Dad found out and he comforted the store owner, who quickly realized he made a big mistake. The story goes the shop owner ran around yelling for help with my Dad following close behind trying to catch him. Shelves, displays, and merchandise knocked over in their wake. The owner had speed on his side that day and was able to escape the grasp of my farther.

For most of my life that small store sat abandoned, I have only vague memories of it even being opened, and I always wondered if that day contributed to its ultimate demise.

Dad was also a walking contradiction; he taught us to respect all races, but frowned on mixed-race relationships. He was uncompromising with us kids when it came to faith and religious education, but only stepped into a church if there was no other choice. He drank a lot, he smoked a lot, and he swore a lot, but he worked hard at keeping us kids from doing the same.

There was another story that my brother Buddy and his friends piled into a coffee shop before school. Without looking at the person sitting next to him at the bar, Buddy asked if they had a smoke. The person said yes and Buddy turned to the smiling face of Dad.

Buddy told me that even after he was married with a son of his own, he still wouldn't smoke in front of Dad, and Dad never gave his permission to do so. Buddy explained that in Dad's logic if he didn't give permission to smoke, you would smoke less.

SUNDAY DINNER

Sunday dinners were mandatory. It didn't matter if you had a date, ball game, or were married with kids of your own. You had to be at the house for Sunday dinner, no exceptions. Mom cooked the gruel all week, and some of those meals were pretty bad, but Dad handled Sunday dinner and for a six-foot-something tough guy, he was a decent enough cook.

Dad made Sunday dinners an art, and Sunday mornings I sat slopping up my cereal, eyes still crusted with sleep, watching him in that mad rage with the potato peeler. It was like his one-size-fits-all cooking tool; he used it on everything. I swear he did an entire dinner with a potato peeler and a small knife.

I remember my milk-splattered chin quivering at the thought of getting close to those large gorilla arms swinging side to side in a relentless destruction of those poor vegetables. I sat terrified his hand would fall on my head and within minutes I would be peeled, quartered, and dropped with the rest of the chunks of potatoes, carrots, and squash in that ever-present pot of murky water.

It was scary, but comforting. It brought a certain structure to our lives, and without any of us knowing it, this became a connection to memories of him that would have otherwise been lost like the vegetable water circling down the drain.

Sunday began early, with Dad using his clenched fist to bang on the wall separating our townhouse from my Aunt's, who was Dad's sister. Three bangs as he walked down the stairs to get the coffee on. If there was no response in a couple of minutes, there would be another three bangs while he waited for the coffee to brew. This would go on until he heard a bang from the other side so he knew someone was up.

It was always three bangs on the wall; to get everyone up, three bangs. To call Aunty over when the coffee was ready, three bangs. If my cousins got too loud or were fighting, three bangs. There was actually a crack, zig-zagging from floor to ceiling on my Aunt's side of the wall blamed on the years of my father's banging.

My Aunt once told me she was sick one morning and couldn't get out of bed. Tossing and turning all night, she had just fallen asleep when Dad banged on the wall, *bang, bang, bang*, snapping her back awake. She thought she could just ignore it, but moments later, *bang, bang, bang*, and she knew Dad wouldn't stop, so she picked up a shoe and tossed it at the wall and missed.

Bang, bang, bang, her hand fell onto a book and flung it towards the wall, but still came up short.

Bang, bang, bang, she tried to yell but it caused a coughing fit.

Bang, bang, bang, she looked for something, anything, that would reach the wall and make enough noise so Dad would stop, and she spotted the bedside lamp and wondered.

Bang, bang, bang, it was from her side of the wall. One of her sons had finally gotten up and answered Dad's alarm.

IS THIS WHAT LOVE IS

Mom and Dad didn't sleep together; Dad had his room, and Mom camped out on the couch, or on one of the bunk beds in the boys' room. I vaguely remember babysitters, but I'm not sure they went out together; Mom loved BINGO, and Dad loved to socialize with a beer or two. I don't remember them hugging, holding hands, or ever showing anything like true affection.

My older siblings may have memories of PDA moments, but to me they seemed to not like each other much. There were incidents, like the time Dad came home with a gushing wound on his head, or when Mom fell to the kitchen floor, but these times confused me more than anything else.

Fate always seemed to place me in the wrong spot at the right time, and I was once again sitting at the table, front row for an evening of bickering and name-calling.

This argument had something to do with Mom's revenge over another argument they had a couple days before. It seemed Mom was still pissed about the argument-- losing the argument or even winning the argument. She was just pissed, and when she was pissed, she became mean.

To get back at Dad for whatever, she soaked his underwear in bleach.

I'm not sure of the formula of her deed: I don't know if she washed them in pure bleach, a higher bleach-to-water ratio, or dipped them in bleach. All I know is Dad worked in construction, and his job was outside, hot, sweaty, and labor intensive, and by the time he got home that day, from his waist to his knees was a big rash that was raw and painful. He was fuming and Mom was pretty pleased with herself.

Dad was at his throne, the chair at the end of the table, and I was at the other end while Mom was at the stove stirring something bubbling in a pot. There was a crash as the spoon hit the floor, then a thud as Mom hit the floor and her body began to violently shake. It seemed Dad was out of the chair and at her side before she landed, reaching in his back pocket for his wallet.

"Someone help!" he yelled, as he pried Mom's mouth open and jammed his wallet in between her jaws.

I was frozen, horrified at my mother's shaking body and my father trying to hold her. He looked lost, helpless, and scared. I think seeing Dad, my big, tough father, look so scared and helpless shut down my memory. Help came, but I don't remember who or how. I do remember thinking through all the bullshit, all the arguments and dirty tricks, my Dad really did love this woman. It was on his face as he tried to comfort her.

THE DREAM

His dream was to have a home of his own, a farm house with a little taste of land somewhere in the country. He wasn't looking for forty acres and a mule; just a place to call his own, a place with enough space to grow some peppers, and tomatoes, and maybe a squash or two. Something tangible to touch, see, and point at to show all his hardships were worth it.

The reason he moved into a low-income housing project is now lost with time and the deaths of his generation. Whatever the reason, I'm sure he never expected to be trapped there for almost two decades. I'm sure he never expected his life to end without so much as touching any of his dreams. I'm sure he never expected Mom's emotional problems to grow worse.

I'm sure he thought he had plenty of time.

He left this earth with the tired soul and worn body of a working man whose dreams lay unfulfilled, but he left in his wake the sense of pride, respect, and hard work in all of us.

Yes, he died a young man, but he also lived a long life.

I DON'T REMEMBER HUGS

I went to Bingo with Mom once, just once. It was held in what use to be my elementary school, but now was the community center for the church. We sat at long tables in the auditorium, one Bingo card in front me. I noticed everyone, including my Mom, had a dozen or more cards in front of them, and was convinced they were looking at me with pity. Their eyes screaming 'amateur'.

When they called the first number, I heard an immediate 'tap, tap, tap' next to me as my mother quickly dabbed the number off all her cards. I struggled to keep up, struggled to find each number called on my one card.

I never went back.

THE VOICE INSIDE HER HEAD

She only listens to the voice inside her head,
It's the only voice she trusts.
It is her dark sister, her shadow twin,
And it walks the narrow streets of her fractured mind,
In its hands carrying a gray, wooden box.
Inside the box is the girl's emotions, feelings, and her heart.
All she ever was, all she is, all she will ever be.
It's to keep her safe, the dark twin says.
Keep me safe, the girl agrees.
Now all she has to do in life is listen to
Her dark twin,
The voice inside her head.

NANA AND GRANDPA

Mom's dad, Joseph Francis Henry Bedard, etched out a decent 'working-class' living as a machinist in a local tool shop, and this immigrant from Quebec, Canada supplemented the family with a fairly large backyard garden. He incorporated a lot of the 'old ways', and lived what today we would call a somewhat self-sufficient lifestyle. His children and grandchildren share memories of the short, balding man, smiling his toothless grin, teaching them how to pinch tomato plants, weed the flower beds, and safely handle poison ivy.

There are countless memories of Grandpa showing how to efficiently remove periwinkles from the rocks along the Cape Cod Canal. He showed them how to steam the periwinkles in seasoned water, and use a sewing needle to pluck out the chewy pea-sized nugget and pop it into their mouths.

They still see him in his white 'wife-beater' undershirt working in the yard, or the white button-down shirt he seemed to always wear when he was in public. They remember the countless games of checkers in which he hummed consistently and would drum his fingers loudly on the table as you tried to think out your next move.

It was a distraction, and it worked because he rarely lost.

He was married to Catharine Mary Fitzgerald whose early life is a mystery to most. She was born in Taunton, Mass in 1898 to Edward and Mary Fitzgerald. As a baby she was taken away when her parents were accused as being alcoholics and sent to a children's home run by nuns. It was under this strict Catholic discipline that she was raised, and even when she came of age she stayed under the nun's care until she met the man who would be her husband.

Known in the family as Nana, she also contributed to passing down some of the old ways to the next generations. Today, a couple decades after her passing, her recipe for canning an old style of piccalilli is still sought after, and a new generation is being introduced to 'Nana and Grampa' through memories in the stories and food still passed around the family.

There was no denying that Joseph ran the house; in their later years he did most of the cooking, the shopping, the cleaning, and the yard work, but Nana ruled the roost. Most days she held court from her favorite chair in the living room, dressed in her one of her flowered house dresses and the black thick-soled shoes common to the nuns that she also preferred.

She kept her hair short, in the style of 30s housewife. No one knows how her right eye was damaged-- the eye turned within so only the white showed-- but her warm features and genuine smile she had for her grandchildren made you forget about it. For her children, and everyone else, she had a quiet observation of all around her that gave off an air of authority, and sent the message: "Do not step out of line."

It was a trait she passed down to her only daughter.

They had stopped at a local store after church service, Joseph went inside for the Sunday paper and a cigar. After a moment, Catharine turned to the young boy, her grandson, in the back seat.

"Go inside," she said. "Make sure your grandfather is not flirting with that young girl behind the counter."

She was serious.

Joseph and Catharine brought forth four sons; Raymond in 1926, Adelard in 1928, Francis in 1929 and Joseph in 1931. But it wasn't until their fifth child that the dynamics of the family changed. It was the beginning of family divisions, some that lasted generations, and family separations that ended only after death.

The baby was born on August 17, 1932 and given the same name as her mother; Catharine Mary Bedard, but through her life she was known as Kay. Her first few years of life were spent in an apartment at 16 Terrace Street in Boston, Massachusetts, and sometime during her early years she moved to a small house on a dead-end street in the sleepy farm town of Foxboro, just south of the city.

Her childhood is as much a mystery as her mother's. There are stories of special treatment that caused some bad sibling blood, and being the youngest and only girl, the beginnings of a problem Kay had with other females that found themselves caught within her small circle. This began to show itself when her brothers introduced other women into the family, and carried over to her daughters-in-law. By far, the worst of her wrath was saved for her own daughter.

When asked, a sister-in-law would only say that Kay and her mother when teamed up were not so nice, and an overwhelming force to contend with. She added that Kay always seemed to be a very unhappy person.

Maybe it was because, not unlike the mother-in-law she never knew, she also left the comfortable middle-class in exchange for low income housing and a lifetime of struggle. Maybe it was the battle with epilepsy and the less-than-side-effect-free medication she was on. Maybe it was living with six children in a small three-bedroom townhouse with no money and no future prospects. Maybe her mental illness and spoiled upbringing left her unable to cope with even the smallest of life's inconveniences.

Beyond that, there is nothing on record to explain the emotional struggle Kay had, not only with people in general, but with her own children.

A BAD MOOD LOOKING FOR AN EXCUSE

It was a few miles round-trip Kay had to walk to get to the grocery store, a few miles juggling heavy bags by herself. She was already in a mood that day and the dark rain clouds overhead are promising her trip home will not be a pleasant one.

Kay struggles with the bags, and as the rain begins to fall, her mood only worsens.

With a lucky glance she notices a car passing by, and inside is a young gentleman she recognizes as someone who came to the house once to pick her daughter Maryellen up. The two dated once, maybe twice. It was some time ago, but she recognizes him nonetheless.

He, on the other hand, doesn't even notice her and continues driving on his way.

Her bad mood changes to blind rage.

By the time she makes it home, the rage has overshadowed any rational emotions of right and wrong. Her body overheating with the pressure of adrenaline racing through her veins, she can only think that she needs to unleash it, needs to stop the roar of blood rushing past her ears. Nothing else matters at that point. She doesn't see the other children scrambling out of her way, doesn't hear the voices trying to get her attention.

She has a focus now; she knows what she needs to do, and races up the stairs.

At the top of the stairs she turns a sharp right, past the small bedroom that five of her six children sleep in, past the short hallway that leads to her husband's bedroom, and straight on to the even smaller bedroom of her daughter.

Her face is now contorted in anger. She doesn't knock, she doesn't wait to be invited in, she lets the rage take control and bursts through the door, slamming it shut behind her. The force is hard enough to rattle the obscene religious statue hanging from the wall a short distance away.

Immediately the yelling starts, quickly followed by the screaming.

There may have been a heavy rain that day, may have been a torn bag and some spilled groceries; then again, there may have only been a bad mood looking for an excuse. Maybe it had nothing to do with an old boyfriend not stopping to give her a ride home in the rain. There are a number of versions of this story, all of them different, all weirdly the same, but all involving just two people: Kay and her daughter.

The only absolute is the young boy hiding under his blankets against the violent noises coming from the closed door down the hall.

There were two things Kay could not tolerate: another woman living in her home, and any of her children outwardly being disloyal to her. As a Daddy's girl, Maryellen started off with two strikes against her and was the go-to for Kay when she was angry. Kay was physical with only Maryellen; none of the boys faced the beatings.

When the young boy gets home from school the following afternoon, he is told his sister ran away.

A RARE, LOVING MOMENT

It was a shift in the silence that woke me up, because even in the middle of the night there was always some kind of noise in the house. There was always a television or radio on, wall-shaking snoring from my father's room, or my mother pacing the hallway talking to the Father, Son, and Holy Ghost. You got used to it, became deaf to it, and wore it like a comforting blanket.

That night there was something different, something more than the lack of sleep farts coming from my brother Tommy on the top bunk. A silence had replaced the nightly noise, and it was like walking out into a yard full of chirping crickets that you didn't notice until they become silent all at once. It was an alien quiet which snatched me from the contented sleep that only a young boy can reach.

Now wide awake, my bladder began telling me it has no shame and will begin releasing in 10, 9, 8... and that was enough for me to get out of bed. My trip back from the bathroom took me by the top of the stairs, and that was when I heard quiet murmurs coming from the kitchen. A conversation trying to take place in hushed tones that on any other night I wouldn't have noticed, but that was enough for me to sneak down.

There was a titanic-sized television in the living room against the bottom section of the stairs. It gave pretty good cover if you were able to avoid the middle steps that creaked like a bastard. Leaning around the wood-like veneer gave you a dead-on view into the kitchen. It was a straight line to the sink where I saw my father leaning his head under the running facet. I could see the clear water turning pink as it ran down his face, and the top part of his shirt drenched in what I knew was blood.

I was frozen. I'd never seen that much blood before and although there was a growing fear for my father's well-being, he was talking, moving his head around. He looked OK.

What horrified me more was what my mother was doing.

My siblings and I learned early on that *Happy Days*, *The Brady Bunch*, and *The Partridge Family* were not us. Even the show *Good Times* about a poor family, like us, living in a low-income project, like us, was not us. The difference was with Mom. We are the poster children that prove not all women are maternal, not all women are meant to be moms, and not all moms offer love unconditionally.

I just figured she wasn't hard-wired that way.

As I peered from behind the casket-sized television, I saw that one of her hands was cupped under the faucet, guiding the water gently over his head, while the fingers of her other hand brushed the blood gently from his hair. Her head slightly tilted, a soft, soothing hum coming from her lips, a look of motherly contentment on her face.

I hate to admit that it scared the shit out of me.

I had never seen her before, or since, be that loving, that tender and caring. I have seen that look thousands of times on my wife's face, but this was the only time I saw it on my mother.

I guess it's why it burnt itself into my memory.

It took over forty years for me to find out what really happened. I was sitting in my brother's backyard one summer night with my feet by a fire and fingers around a cold beer, just two brothers remembering our version of the glory days.

He explained that Dad was the tough guy everyone looked for; some idiot loses a fight with his wife and heads to the bar to drink the pissed-off out of his system, and is always looking for some tough guy to sucker punch their man-hood back.

On that night, this guy just picked the wrong person.

Dad was sitting at the bar at the Ward 5 Club that night. The owner was tending bar and it was just he and Dad until some guy walked in looking for a fight. The story is the guy, without saying a word, picked up a thick glass ashtray from one of the tables and slammed it into Dad's forehead.

Years later, I can only imagine the look on this guy's face after expecting my Dad to be knocked out cold on the floor, but finding him only dazed, bloody, but very much sitting up and aware.

Before the poor, misguided fool knew what happened, he was on the floor, Dad on top of him swinging those massive arms into that poor bastard's head.

My brother said that Dad was pounding on this guy so hard and viciously that the bartender had to rush around with a baseball bat to try and stop it.

"He was scared Dad was going to kill the guy," my brother told me. "He yelled, 'Bob so help me God if you don't get off that guy I will bash your head in with this bat!'"

50

Nobody knows what the guy's name was, or what happened to him that night. Dad went home to the very rare embrace of my mother, and the man was left in the bartender's hands.

DO YOU REMEMBER HUGS?

At this point in my life, my mother and I have gone our separate ways. We exchange hellos at family events, if she phones, most times I answer the call, but our roles as mother and son no longer exist.

My limit with Mom came on the night a man with a gun came to my house looking for me. I was at work, but my wife and three young children were home, alone, scared and confused by this man ranting angerly at our front door.

It seems Mom was convinced I was going to discover something about my brother Billy and she was worried about how I was going to react; to this day I don't know what that something is, nor does Billy, and I don't care to find out, but my mother's broken mind shot into high gear, and all she could think of was protecting her youngest son at all cost.

Her warped way of thinking came up with the plan to call the father of the young girl that babysat for my brother's kids. She told this man, who didn't know us, that I was going to hurt his daughter and she wanted to warn him before I do.

I don't blame the guy, I would have reacted the same way, but I tracked him down the next day and was able to calm him down. I was able to convince him I had no idea what I was suppose to be so mad about, I didn't know his daughter and had no plans to harm her or anyone else.

Even though I averted this crisis, a burning thought began to grow in my head; what if I was home that night, what if this man just opened fire as the door opened, what if he sat in his car and waited for me.

I decided then to divorce my mother.

The one thing about my mother's mental illness is it leaves her with no guilt, no sense of wrong doing. Her mind not only allows her to justify her actions, it also in some cases wipes the event clean from her memory. This is why I didn't bring anything specific up when we talked.

It was simple; "You don't like me, and I'm having a hard time with that, and it's causing issues for both of us. I think it would be best if we stop being mother and son and go our separate ways."

With out debate or protest, she agreed.

Simple, uneventful, classic Mom.

A few years later one of my brothers asked if it was time for me to get over it.

"She's still your mother, you know," he said. "She's getting older and not going to be here much longer. How will you feel then?"

He's right of course.

Yes, I will be sad when Mom dies, and it will neither surprise nor shock me to feel the wet streaks of tears running down my cheeks. The only problem is the sadness and tears will not be for the loss of a mother, but for the loss of what could have been and now will never be.

That, I think, will be the hardest for me to take.

"Do you remember any hugs?" I asked my brother.

At the time I didn't really know why I asked that; it wasn't anything I was thinking about, wasn't weighing on my mind. Maybe it was just my way of trying to justify my decision to divorce a parent.

"Just one memory of when Mom hugged you?" I asked again.

He looked at me blankly, eyes squinting slightly as his thoughts dug into the deepest corners trying to drum up something, anything, but I could see by the sudden change in his expression he was coming up cold.

We both quickly changed the subject.

I did ask the same question to my adult children, some co-workers, and a couple guys at a social club where I would partake in a cold alcoholic beverage from time to time. In each case I was giving examples, moments that stood out above the rest that brought out that slow, soft smile spreading across their faces.

It has always eluded me on how it must feel to have a mother's hug chase away the whispers of a bad dream, ease the ache of a skinned knee, or show the love and pride she had in her heart after a life-changing event.

I don't remember hugs.

I don't remember hand-holding as we strolled down the street.

I don't remember the comforting feel of hands softly holding my cheeks as she told me everything was going to be alright.

I don't remember ever feeling the safe embrace of a mother's unconditional love towards her child.

I cannot be confident that maternal moments are not hidden somewhere, buried deep within my subconscious. If so, they are overshadowed by the sharp edges of emotional abuse that is the thread of my mother's relationship with her children.

THE FINGER

The front door had what we called a mail slot in it. It was just a small, rectangular metal flap just below the center of the door that the mailman could push any letters though. This was long before Amazon, so most of what you got was bills, letters, and store catalogs; the weekly store flyers came tucked inside the Sunday paper.

Sometimes the Avon lady would push her hand through the slot to open it and yell, "Kay! Kay, are you there?" if no one opened the door fast enough.

At the end of the month, as soon as the tinny squeak from the rusted springs of the flap, and the flutter of envelopes hitting the floor sang out, Mom was on the pile. She would weed out any bills, specifically utility bills, and respectfully she at least opened and glanced at them. I'm not sure what she was hoping to see because she would quickly tear them into small pieces and dump the shreds into the trash. If the bill was especially interesting she would flush the torn pieces down the toilet.

In her fractured mind she figured that if the bills didn't exist, she didn't have to pay them. To be honest, I thought it had more to do with not letting Dad see a bill that he gave her money to pay, but she didn't.

There were far too many times I came home from school and found extension cords coming up from the cellar, which was on the Housing Authority circuit, fed through the kitchen window and hooked up to various appliances because power was shut off. There was an equal amount of times we would run back and forth from my Aunt's apartment to take or place calls because our phone was shut off.

This usually ended in Mom and Dad arguing, and I found myself, once again, in the front row for what was the worst of these.

Dad worked in concrete forms; this was the art of building and setting up heavy wooden forms that molded concrete into walls for new homes. It was mostly done from late spring to very early fall, and was a dirty, hot job.

I see him sitting at the end of the kitchen table, his right arm resting on the top, his left hand resting on his left leg. He was still in his work clothes: weather-worn leather boots, faded concrete-splattered jeans, and a yellow tank top that covered his large frame and even larger 'beer' belly. His face, now shaved for the summer with just a mustache left, was looking down to the floor. He looked hot, tired, and at that moment, defeated.

Something was shut off, something that Dad gave Mom money to pay, but she didn't and he asked why.

If she had just answered the question, blamed it on a mistake or even told Dad, "None of your fucking business," the events would have been much different. Instead, she began this verbal barrage on every bad thing Dad had said or done, ever. Her mouth vomited out every possible insult, every degrading remark that she knew would hit the right buttons. All the time, she was waving her right index finger at him.

During all this he said nothing, kept his face down, and did what he'd done for most of their marriage: took his wife's bullshit. Except this time, there was a point crossed.

Dad slowly lifted his head up, looked at Mom, and spoke.

"If you wave that finger in my face one more time I'm going to break it off."

There was nothing scary or threatening about it. In fact, it was more tired and sad, which may have been why my mother felt confident to push the argument to the next level. She leaned into him, her index finger almost touching his nose, and with that *fuck you* look I've seen on her face many times, she waved that finger.

It was quick; Dad's hand came up and before Mom could react, he grabbed her finger and twisted it up, just as quickly let it go, and pushed himself away from the table. Mom screamed and ran to the other side of the kitchen holding her finger in her hands while Dad walked out, went up the stairs to the bathroom, and ran the water for his bath.

Her finger wasn't broken off; it wasn't broken at all. There was no sprain, no bruise. She was shocked more than hurt, although Dad did give it a painful twist.

Sometime while Dad was getting his bath ready, Mom called the police, and two officers showed up at the door within a few minutes. I was beginning to feel horrified; I wasn't happy with Dad twisting Mom's finger, even if she was the one who instigated it, but I was getting the feeling this was on the verge of being out of control.

Mom played the wounded wife role to the officers and they both walked up the stairs. I heard a knock on a door, some muffled voices, and moments later footsteps coming down the stairs. One officer was in front, one in the back, and Dad was handcuffed in the middle of them. He was now shirtless and his work pants were beltless and unbuckled. The officer behind him was at first hanging onto the back of Dad's pants, keeping them from falling down.

Outside, a small crowd began to gather; I remember my cousin Bobby Sheehan and his brother Will, and my Aunt. I think my brother Buddy was there, also. This was the era before cable and video games, so police coming out of an apartment with someone in cuffs was enough to bring a crowd, but Dad was also popular on the street and the growing crowd was getting very vocal.

I'm sure the officers were a bit unsettled and forgot all about Dad's pants, which kept falling to his knees, and the crowd got louder. Just as another cruiser squealed to a stop, my cousin Bobby jumped in front of the officers demanding they let him at least buckle his Uncle's pants up. The words no sooner left his lips and he was tackled, cuffed, and tossed in the back of the second cruiser.

The crowd was now on the verge of rushing the police, and they quickly got Dad in the back of the other cruiser and both cruisers drove off.

The anger now turned to my mother.

I don't remember how or when my Dad and my cousin returned home, but I remember the moments after they were taken away.

Mom closed and latched all the windows and doors, trapping my brother Billy and I in an apartment in the peak of summer with no fans or ventilation. I sneaked a peek out the backdoor window and saw two women helping my Aunt back to her apartment. I could tell she was crying.

"You red-headed bitch!" she yelled towards our windows, and I ducked back out of view.

A FRACTURED MIND

She may have had dreams once. Maybe as a young girl running in the tall grass along the country road she called home, she may have dreamed of a storybook wedding and a happily-ever-after life. Maybe she dreamed of becoming a famous artist and traveling the world, meeting all her adoring fans. Maybe she just dreamed of being happy, about something, anything.

By the time I came into the world she was already beaten down by life, already stripped of any hopes or dreams. Her fractured mind was unable to see anything but unhappiness and anger at those around her. She could only hear one voice, and that was the dark voice inside her head.

A TALE OF TWO PARENTS

BLURRED LINES

Yesterday's young mind
Absorbing the onslaught of ideas,
until a new mix of opinion is formed;
Greatly influenced
By an orchestra of voices.
Today's simple mind
Is nothing more
Then blurred lines of right and wrong.

THE CANDY STORE HEIST

The name of the store eludes me at this stage of my life, and I'm sure it's hidden under a dead brain cell somewhere. In my later teens it was a fireplace store that also sold fishing bait, a weird combo, I agree, but early on I remember it as a Mom-and-Pop type shop that sold penny candies actually for a penny.

It was located across from the entrance of the street, on the hill section that gave the street its name. It had a red brick storefront that butted out of a two-story apartment house I always assumed the old couple that ran it lived in. There was also a three-step cement stairway that ran the length of the building with a sheet metal awning hanging over it.

Inside the store was small and cluttered with shelves of impulse items such as milk and breads, and overpriced canned goods. Most of us still got our milk and juices delivered by the actual Milkman, but most of us also forgot to pay him from time to time, so having a place to get a quick gallon was more than convenient.

The floors were those wide, wooden boards that creaked under your feet and gave the place an old, earthy smell that was only slightly offensive when you were 8 or 9, but as an adult brought a flood of memories and a smile.

I don't remember who came up with the idea, but when my friend James, his younger brother, and I walked through the door, a plan was already in place. Basically, James's brother was going to distract the old guy behind the counter while James and I filled our pockets with candy. A simple plan; no moving parts and straight to the point.

Even with Dad keeping a firm hand on all of us Barry boys, none of us were angels; this wasn't the first act of crime I had committed, and was far from the last. Yet, I could never figure out how guys who did this kind of thing all the time could be so calm about it.

Just walking up to the door, I was terrified.

I remember walking in the store trying to act as casual as possible, and failing miserably at it. Beads of sweat began to pool along my forehead, and I could feel sweat race down the back of my neck. My hands were shaking so badly I had to cross my arms and shove my hands under my pits to stop it. James, on the other hand, was already in the candy aisle pulling items off the shelf as calmly as if he were taking a pair of socks out of his bureau drawer.

His brother had the old guy searching for some bogus can of vegetables, and I was too focused on shoving chocolate squirrels, red hot balls, and Bazooka Bubble Gum into my jeans pockets. My entire body was jamming with so much nervous energy that I almost screamed when James tugged on my arm and motioned his head toward the door.

With each step, I fully expected an old, contorted hand to fall on my shoulders, yank me back into the store, and a wrinkled angry face cover me with spittle as the old man yelled obscenities and threats. I don't think it was until we got out of the store and across the street before my heart began to settle and I could breathe again.

James and I hid behind some bushes waiting for his brother, and as he crossed the street I could see the old man through the store window watching us, then walking around the aisle James and I were in looking confused and concerned. For a moment I felt bad, the Catholic guilt trying to grab hold and pull itself to the surface. It almost succeeded, until James handed me a root beer barrel hard candy and the instant sugar rush pushed the guilt back down to where it belonged.

The plan was to wait until we got to the rock to divide up the bounty.

The rock was at the far corner of the project section of the street, behind the back field. We called it the rock because, well, it was a rock. It protruded up out of the ground about three feet, was a good two 'asses' wide, and long enough to seat three people on each side. It was just some random boulder left behind by the builders, but it offered the perfect vantage point for whatever shenanigans you were involved in.

Sitting on the rock, in front of you was the basketball court, and beyond that the open field that ran the length of the street. To the right gave you a panoramic view of the entire projects so no one could approach without you seeing, and to the left was a path that went through the back fence into a small patch of woods and to the abutting street.

The fence here had been broken so many times that the Housing Authority eventually gave up and left that section of fence open. The rock sat back just enough so you would see anyone coming down that path long before they saw you.

The back of the rock abutted another chain link fence that looked onto what I thought of as the strangest homestead I'd ever seen. Right there, in the middle of a city and bordering a low-income housing project was a small ranch-style house sitting on what I'm guessing was a good half-acre of land. The yard was framed by old shade trees and in the center was a large canopy that was completely engulfed by Concord grape plants.

In the fall, the old couple that owned the property would bag up the grapes and hand them out to all of us kids. Even today, a taste of true Concord grapes, either in juice, jelly, or actual berry, brings me back to that spot.

The best surprise involved the shed tucked away in the far corner. It was nothing more than a renovated tool shed with a door on one end. If you said to yourself it looked a bit like the horse stall from the television show *Mr. Ed*, you would not be far off.

Housed inside the shed was a miniature horse-- I kid you not. If my memory serves me correctly, she was the size of a St. Bernard dog, and had a dark brown coat with a thick blonde mane and tail. My brothers remember when her owners would hitch her to a small carriage for rides, but I only knew of her lazily roaming her property line, waiting for one of us kids to push some grass through the double fence for her to munch on.

I can remember many a summer afternoon sitting on that rock, watching the horse trot around while the old couple escaped the heat of the day sitting under the canopy of grapes. I always dreamed what it must be like to live such a grand life as theirs. Of course, I knew nothing of them-- I didn't even know their names-- but through the eyes of a boy who only knew the life of the projects, theirs looked grand.

James and I emptied out our pockets onto the top of the rock and were amazed at the amount. There had to have been a couple of pounds of prime, brand-named sweets. Even divided three ways, it was more candy than I have ever had at one time; except maybe on Halloween.

I didn't remember walking home and I don't remember falling asleep, but I remember snapping out of my sugar coma when I heard my father's heavy footsteps coming up the stairs.

"What, are you sick?" Dad asked looking through the door.

I was about to answer when I saw his head look down to the bureau I shared with two other brothers and to the pile of candy scattered on top of it. I must have emptied my pockets before I laid down, not thinking anyone would notice; however, the look on my father's face told me that was an epic fail.

"Where did that candy come from?" he asked.

I remember this movie in which a man had undergone some government experiments and ended up with this form of telekinetic power. All this dude had to do was look into your eyes and speak, and your sorry ass was doing anything he told you to do. My father was that man, and without so much as a, "What candy?", I spilled my guts. I told him everything: distracting the owner, filling my pockets, sorting the goods on the rock, and stuffing my face to the point I almost puked.

I told him everything except that there were three of us, not because of any loyalty to my friends, but because my father held us responsible for our own actions, regardless of the roles anyone else may have played. Whatever was about to come down on my head would not be any different if Dad knew there was two other culprits.

Why waste the breath?

The scary part was he became calm after I threw myself at the mercy of the court; he didn't smile or anything, but he didn't yell either. He quietly told me to put my shoes on, gather up what remained of the candy, and follow him.

I wasn't going to argue. I blindly followed.

We went downstairs and he told my mother we would be right back, I was confused, but nodded in agreement and continued to follow.

Out the front door, the beginnings of concern grew and my mind began racing, but I figured, what the hell could happen?

It wasn't until we began walking up the hill and towards the candy store that the terror began to spark.

He was taking me back to the fucking store.

He was going to rat me out to the old guy.

I was going to go to jail and be somebody's boy-toy.

My brain went all zombie on me.

Before I could utter a protest, my father was opening the glass doors and waving me to go in first. My brain was still on autopilot, my body completely under the control of Dad's voice as he commanded me to enter, to walk over to the checkout table, to stand there, and not say a word.

Dad explained to the old guy that I helped myself to some of his candy without paying for it, to which he commanded I put the candy on the table.

He told the shopkeeper that it was a safe bet I had helpers, and that I had eaten a fair amount already. My Dad's solution to this was for me to come to the store each day for the following week and work off the cost of the candy I couldn't return.

I can still see the amused face of the old man as he looked down at me. I was screwed-- royally screwed.

The old guy ended up having some mercy on me. Each day after school, I went to the store for my punishment. Each day the old man gave me a broom and had me sweep for an hour, and each day his wife would send me home with a bag of treats.

Not much longer after that, the store closed. There was no going out of business sale, no retirement announcements, no announcements at all.

One day, the doors were just locked.

FIVE-FINGER DISCOUNT

When you have no car, no real form of transportation, you tend to shop close to home. Your choices are pretty much narrowed down by walking distance. We were lucky that within a couple of miles in any direction, we had a few movie theaters, some grocery stores, produce stands, and numerous fast food joints.

We also had two competing department stores.

In the late 60s and early 70s, department stores were still somewhat new, and just beginning to push out the smaller Mom-and-Pops. For families that were doing pretty good and able to shell out a little more for name brands, there was a store about a mile down the road called Bradlees. The store was bright, clean, and all the aisles were organized with products lined on pretty shelving units. There always seemed to be workers around, not only to follow us hood-rats so we didn't steal, but also to actually help customers.

For the rest of us there was Mammoth Mart, the 60s version of a bargain basement. The store's sign portrayed a smiling elephant dressed in a blazer, shirt, and tie. The elephant was standing with his hand showing off its badge with its mascot name printed on it: Marty.

Ironically, it was located across the street from Bradlees, but the inside was its polar opposite; it was no-frills with exposed fixtures and racks of nothing more than pipes to hang clothes on. Although clean, the place had a dingy feel about it, with less intense lighting than other stores.

The store did make up for its lack of curbside appeal with store-wide events, a first for department stores, at least in our area. Each summer the store would welcome a traveling carnival to set up in the back parking lot for a week. The goal was to have parents let the kids hang out on the rides and fun house while they shopped-- an idea that worked in the 60s when you wouldn't be arrested for leaving your kids in the care of some strange carnival workers.

The store also invited local celebrities for a meet-and-greet with customers. Hockey great Bobby Orr was a regular, and I remember for one event, Mom made my older brothers take me with them; I was maybe five at the time. Once we arrived and stood in line to meet the hockey legend, it didn't take long for all of my brothers to disappear. I'm not talking they went to check out the records, or even flirt with some girls in the clothes aisle; the bastards were gone. They had left the building and went home.

I had no idea at that time how to get home. I was well aware I was surrounded by a crowd of total strangers, and quickly became terrified my face was going to end up on the back of a milk carton. I did what any five-year-old would do in that situation; I found a corner to curl up in and cried.

To this day, I have a phobia of being lost in a strange place.

Eventually, a store employee discovered me and was able to somehow get my name, address, and even a phone number. My clearest memory is Mom dragging me home by my arm, pissed off and swearing. She was upset not that I was left behind, but that she had to stop doing whatever she was doing to come and get me.

I was surprised to learn the Mammoth Mart store had a number of other firsts as well; it was the first full-discount department store in the New England area, the first to offer no-frills interior, the first to have rows of checkout lines at the front of the store, and the first to have off-priced "seconds" in clothes. The "seconds" were mostly name brands that were either last year's styles or more often had minor defects. The company would buy these by the train load and sell them at dirt-cheap prices.

Name brands at a discount is what made the store popular with the Hill Street project moms. Come first day of school, and 9 out of 10 kids in the class were wearing a Mammoth Mart outfit.

Mom was big into the Mammoth Mart discounts as well; only in her case, it was the five-finger kind.

On more than one occasion, she would drag me to Mammoth Mart and station me at the end of an aisle. My job was simple: I was to watch for anyone, employee or otherwise, who was coming our way and warn my mother. While I was standing guard, my mother would be filling her pockets, pocketbook, bra, and girdle with any merchandise that would fit.

She used this same tactic with some of the neighbors: Mom would be having coffee at a neighbor's house when the neighbor would excuse themselves to go to the bathroom. Mom instructed me to signal her when they were returning while she was filling her pocketbook with canned goods.

BLURRED LINES

The blurred lines between right and wrong began early for all of us Barry's; through words and actions, Dad taught the value of having a job; of the financial, emotional, and spiritual rewards from honest hard work; and that nothing in this world is free. I have no memory of Dad ever calling in sick to work, do not remember him leaving a job on the table that was offered to him. Rain or shine, hot or cold, sick or healthy, he went to work every day there was work to go to.

Because of Dad, we were considered "working" poor, and it wasn't until years later that I learned how different that was from my friends who lived in one-parent households supported by welfare and food stamps.

Mom, through her words and actions, taught us the fine art of how to lie yourself out of most situations. By association, we learned to justify taking people's "stuff." Most of all, we learned to lie to, defy, and at some levels even dislike Dad-- for no other reason than he took his role as a parent seriously, and my mother did not.

TWO FOR A DOLLAR

At the beginning of sixth grade, I took one of my brother's old school books, a thick one, and I brushed glue on the outside edges of the pages. When the glue cured, I added another coat of glue, and kept adding until the pages were fully stuck together. I hollowed out the inside of the book by hammering a steak knife into the glued pages, and cut out a square section so the average box of snack cakes could fit inside.

Most mornings before school I would go to a grocery store-- Fernandes Supermarket I think it was called. Most of the kids hit this place so it was always crowded, and I would head right to the aisle where the boxes of snack cakes were.

I would have that big, heavy book tucked under my arm, but visible to anyone who looked in my direction so they saw me going in and going out with it.

When I made my choice, I would quickly flip the front cover open, drop the box of snack cakes in, close the cover, and make my way back to the entrance. Some days I would buy a bag of chips or a candy bar as a further distraction, or I would meld into one of the groups of kids and walk out with them.

At recess, I would keep two of whatever cakes I had and sell the rest. By mid-year even the teachers would check in with me to see what I had, and get their snack before I ran out.

On paper it seems simple: it was easy and the perfect, victimless crime. In reality, I did this on average three times a week for the entire year, and each time as I walked to the doors, my stolen loot tucked firmly under my arm, I was always about to shit myself.

The voice of Dad in my head kept me from getting too comfortable on the wrong side of the line, but Mom's voice helped me justify it: I actually saved a good portion of the money and used it to buy school clothes as I moved from elementary to middle school life.

There you have it; nobody got hurt, I never got caught, I earned some cash to help with school clothes, and everyone got a snack at recess. I also worked very hard at school and got decent grades, at least until I reached high school.

Besides, don't they have insurance to cover things like this?

THE WHITE VAN

Not long after Dad died, I was already a moody little prick and angry at life, but on this particular day my mood was even darker. I really don't remember why, but I'm pretty sure a girlfriend was involved: a fight, a breakup I don't remember except I was in a dark mood, it was hot, and I didn't feel much like walking the rest of the way home.

I stuck out my thumb and tried to hitch a ride.

Not many have seen my temper unleashed; they've witnessed me angry, maybe yell in my "dad voice", or seen what my wife calls my "scary look"; but very few have actually seen my real temper come out.

Not long after my thumb hit the air, a white panel van stopped. There was a driver and another guy in the front seat, and when the sliding door opened, a third guy sitting on a wooden box motioned me in. I climbed in and took a seat on another wooden box that was next to him.

All I can tell you is the three were white, in their mid-to-late 20s, and were on the scruffy side. I couldn't pick them out in a lineup then, and I can't in any detail describe them now. The guy on the box beside me had shoulder-length greasy hair; maybe if washed it would have been brown, and he reeked of body odor and sour milk. The two in front were both wearing do-rags on their heads, jeans, and white shirts, and seemed cleaner than the guy next to me. I remember dirty fingernails, one had no front teeth, and one really liked the word "fuck."

Strange what the mind remembers.

The back of the van had no windows and was empty except for the two boxes my silent new friend and I were sitting on. Yet, there were no warning signals, no imaginary red flags waving, nothing to tell me to keep my guard up. I think my instincts were fogged over by whatever I was pissed off at. So, when Mr. Sour Smell asked for a cigarette, I didn't think anything of it, and reached into my pocket to get him one.

Maybe at that very moment the van took a sharp turn, or maybe the wooden boxes we were sitting on weren't stable, or Mr. Smelly Guy's skinny ass was too weak to pull off whatever they were planning.

When I turned my head away to get the cigarette, the left side of my face was pushed violently to the right, sending sparks across my eyes. Not unlike my Dad years before, the blow did not put me down or knock me out, but the rage that resulted has blinded most of the event from my memory.

I'm pretty sure I blacked out.

When the blood roar in my ears subsided, I was in the front seat driving the van away. In the side view mirror, I saw the three guys rolling around on the sidewalk. Even then I had no memory of what went down, and as I raced down the street, my whole body was shaking, either from the adrenaline or the fear that I couldn't remember.

I kept the van for close to a month, using it every day to drive to work at a furniture refurbishing shop the next town over. At the end of Hill Street was a liquor store that shared a chain link fence with the street. As with all the fences that surrounded the street, sections at each end were cut open so often they gave up trying to fix it. Each night, I parked the van in the back of the store near the broken section of fence.

I was young and dumb but knew enough not to push my luck; I drove to and from work, and occasionally to a store. What I didn't plan on was the van being reported stolen and the liquor store owner reporting what he thought was an abandoned vehicle in his lot. I also didn't plan on leaving my paycheck stub on the floor of the van.

From what I was told, when the van owner discovered I still had the van and was caught with it, he decided to change his story and suddenly remembered he loaned the vehicle to me. I'm no tough guy, and I have no misconceptions that whoever this guy was he was not afraid of me, no matter how badly I lost my temper. He was afraid the cops would find out he and his buddies drove around robbing hitchhikers.

Yes, technically I stole a van, but what would have happened if I hadn't lost my temper and had a split second to get away? They were bad men trying to do bad things.

HILL STREET STRONG

My cousin Bobby Sheehan acknowledged my writing early on. Not long after Dad died, Bobby asked if I could write something to show how, without Dad, the family was fractured. "Family Tree" is what I came up with. A couple decades after writing it, I visited Bobby at his office and saw "Family Tree" framed and hanging behind his desk.

FAMILY TREE

The tree stood tall, strong.
Sprouting a foliage of sparkling green leaves,
That reached into the sky,
Brushing the bottoms of clouds
As they floated slowly by.

New limbs grew
Like fingers reaching out,
Still connected to the life-line of the tree.
Unified, but individual
Fanning branches to the breeze.

The roots, Patriarch of the clan,
Spread out, gripping, feeding
Providing for all.
The protector of the lineage
Until years take its toll.

In age and illness, the roots begin to die.
In their last gasping act
Branches throw seeds to the wind,
Hoping new saplings will grow
As their unity ends.

HILL STREET

It looked more like an Army base than low income housing. It's what we called the projects back then, and today you would call it "the hood."

The barrack-style buildings were nondescript long boxes with particle board siding painted in unexciting earth tones; it was always rumored the siding was asbestos, and with the number of people lost to cancer, it just might have been. They were more two-story townhouses than apartments, six townhouses to each building with three buildings placed in a U-shape. This U-shape was repeated along that side of the street to make up the bulk of the housing.

There was a courtyard in the middle of the U, nothing more than pavement with two small fenced-in square areas at each end, and in the middle was an open area big enough to ride bikes or play a quick game of kickball. The fenced-in areas were strung with ropes to hang out clothes, and there always seemed to be a mom yelling at us because we were riding our bikes around the wet jeans, or a muddy kickball bounced off someone's clean sheets.

Across the street, the buildings were lined end to end, as if forming a barricade-like force from the small patch of woods that secluded the street from that side. I can remember racing my bike along the walkway that ran the length of the back of these buildings. Most people on this side of the street hung out on their front steps; there was almost nobody in the back. This gave you an almost obstruction-free straight run to go as fast as your legs could pedal.

One hundred units, one hundred families, one hundred different stories.

The inside of the townhouses were for basic accommodations: the bare comforts of keeping warm and dry. The first floor had two rooms; what we called the living room that had a couch, Dad's recliner, and a rocking chair. There was just enough room for the furniture-sized television; when this broke down it became the table for the smaller televisions that came after. We were the first apartment in the unit, number 71-A, so we had windows on the end wall, and the stairs that led up to the second floor took up most of the wall that separated us from the next unit on the other end of the room.

73

An opening led into an eat-in kitchen; small and just barely functional. There was an electric stove, a refrigerator/freezer unit, a metal-based table with a chipped Formica top, and six chairs surrounding it. The chairs matched the table's metal skeleton, and had red plastic seats, several of them with black "duck tape" keeping the yellowed foam from spilling out. To the side of the kitchen was a closet-sized space that had rough-cut shelves and led to the back door. Some families used this as a mud room, and others, like us, used the space as a pantry.

On the other side of the kitchen was a similar space, but this was closed off by a door. Inside, the walls slanted downwards due to the stairs above it, and for most of my childhood this was a junk closet. In my early teens, I dabbled in photography and used this space as a dark-room.

The wall looking out to the back had green painted cabinets that I remember had a few doors with broken hinges so they almost fell off when you opened them. There was a counter with the same chipped Formica top and a basic one-bay white enamel sink. That was the kitchen of my childhood.

Upstairs began with the bathroom at the top of the stairs. Again, basic accommodations with a white enameled pedestal sink, toilet, and tub. In my early years there was no shower, but in my teens, there was a shower adaptor installed by one of my brothers: a simple gadget with the shower head screwed into the wall, and a hose that ran down and slipped over the faucet.

I seem to remember a chest just outside the bathroom. Old, but large enough to hide a person inside. On the outside, it looked more like a pirate's chest, and when opened it smelled of cedar. I remember it being a big letdown; it looked so cool like it should be filled with gold, jewels, and stolen loot, but it was filled with only blankets and old photos.

Next to the bathroom was one of the three bedrooms. It was no more than 15 feet by 15 feet, and at one time had two bunk beds and a crib strategically arranged inside. I remember a four-drawer bureau tucked inside a bump-in that was supposed to be an open closet, and I do believe we all shared this because I know I had at least one drawer all to myself.

Before marriages and boot camps split the family up, the room was arranged with one set of bunks on the far wall, with Tommy on the top bunk and me on the bottom. On the other side of the room was the second bunk with Buddy on the top and Joey on the bottom, and in the middle of us was Billy in the crib.

"Five boys in one room," my wife said once, "I can't even imagine what it must have smelled like."

I didn't understand at first; I agree Mom was never one to push personal hygiene on us. I'm not sure I even owned a toothbrush until I was in my teens. We were not the cleanest kids on the block, but we were clean enough.

Then I began to think about it. I don't remember a regular change of sheets; in fact, my brain sees days when I went to bed with just a mattress and a blanket- - no sheets at all. It wasn't until I moved in with my wife that I even knew what a top sheet was. There was no spring cleaning of the bedrooms, no airing out rooms; if you had a sheet on your bed it was there for a long period of time. Add to this the daily onslaught of boys farting, and the mounds of sweaty socks and underwear, and I began to understand what my wife meant.

I don't remember the rooms, or the house in general, being overly dirty or smelly; then again, I could have been nose-blind to it all.

The upstairs hallway was small and L-shaped, the main section about 14 feet long, and watching over it was part-shrine, part-statue, and part-religious obsession. It was a foot-high statue of Jesus, complete with extended hands and feet with bloody holes in them. The statue was set inside a shrine that was enclosed in glass and framed out in wood. The bottom of the shrine was a six-inch door that folded out on small chains, exposing a compartment that held a number of glass jars supposedly filled with holy water.

At the end of the main hall was the smallest room in the house. This began as my sister's room, and when she left for good, it was passed down to the oldest boy, unless there was an extended house guest. Dad never denied helping someone who was down on their luck, and from time to time we would have a guest living with us.

Other than that, it was a pretty big deal to get your own room-- at least it was for Buddy, Joey and Tommy. By the time the room was open to me, it was only Billy and I in the house anyway, so I focused the excitement on being in a new room.

Although it was the smallest, I always considered it to be the best room in the house. There was just enough space for a single bed, my own bureau, and the coolest closet space ever. Like in the other bedrooms, it was an open-faced closet, except the floor of this space was built up about three feet. I'm guessing it had to do with the upwards slant in the floor because it was over the stairs.

The why didn't matter, because it was a cool little nook where you could lay blankets and pillows down and climb into, and just kill a few hours reading or listening to music. I also discovered that the position of the closet to the door kept you out of sight if someone came into your room and you were cuddled up inside.

The end board of the nook's floor could be lifted up, exposing what I first thought was a great hiding place. I soon learned after I hid money in there that my mother also knew of this space. After the second time the money went missing, I shut it down.

Years later, I learned some of my brothers also knew of the hiding spot, and also learned soon after that Mom knew of it as well.

The "L" section of the hallway was only about 8 feet long and ended at Dad's bedroom. There can be a debate on the size of the "boys'" room or Dad's, but both were close in size. At one point, Dad had a smaller television in this room, and on Friday nights or Saturday mornings I would hunker down in the big bed and watch either horror movies or early morning cartoons. Dad got up early even on weekends, and Mom either slept on the couch or in one of the empty bunk beds, so even when most of my brothers were home it was like having my own space.

After Dad died, I took this room for a couple of reasons: mostly because I needed space for the second-hand drum set I had purchased. It was a gold sparkled Ludwig six-piece kit. It was old, hard to keep in tune, but it was cheap enough for me to buy. The cymbals were all a no-name brand with cracks and dents that made them sound only slightly better than fingernails on a chalkboard.

I pissed off not only the household but most of the neighbors with my constant practicing; at one point, a neighbor started a petition to get either the drums or me removed from the street, and even brought it to my house for my mother to sign. I have no idea if Mom signed it, but I always had a suspicion she did. Some of the other Hill Street moms had a heart-to-heart with this neighbor and she decided to drop the petition.

I will admit here for the first time that some of my practice sessions were actually just me cleaning my pot. I discovered if you titled the snare drum up a little and dumped your bag of pot at the top, all you needed to do was tap the skins with your drumstick and the vibration would cause the seeds to roll down to the bottom. A practice and cleaned pot at the same time; I thought it was genius.

The other reason I took the room was that my Mom pushed me to it. She was convinced my Dad's spirit was still in that room and she wanted nothing to do with it. It became the safest place from Mom's prying eyes and sticky fingers, and in the three years I was in that room, Mom never came in. She really had major emotional and religious issues with the room.

I was lying in bed, headphones on, reading a book. From the corner of my eye, I saw movement and looked towards the bedroom door. An arm was sticking in, my mother's arm, and it was grasping a small glass bottle. Before I could react, the arm began shaking, splashing out the clear liquid that was in the bottle. When the bottle was empty the arm disappeared and the door slammed shut.

This played out more times than I could track; this was Mom splashing holy water, either to drive out the demons in the room, drive out the demons in me, or both.

Except for a handful of units with an extra bedroom, and some one-bedroom units for the elderly, this was the makeup of the street. Some had better furniture, some would be considered hoarder houses, but this was the street.

Hill Street was a meat-and-potatoes type of place: there were no taco Tuesdays or pizza Fridays. Most freezers were filled with the throw-away cuts from the butcher you could get for pennies on the dollar, or cabinets filled with commodity foods from the local church. This meant beef stew with beef tongue as the main ingredient, meat so tough it took days of cooking before you could even chew it. There was also yellow cheese that came in an arm-sized block wrapped in an oily dark brown cardboard box. The cheese was hard, dry, but palpable once you shaved the mold off the edges.

I have to admit it made some good grilled cheese sandwiches.

My favorite commodity food was the peanut butter. It came in an industrial-sized metal container with the ingredients printed in block letters on the outside of the can; no fancy labels on that bad boy. The can itself took some skill to get open without cutting a deep gash in a finger or two. Inside was an epoxy-like mixture that used to be peanut butter, but after years of sitting around was now a hard chunk of clay topped off with two or more inches of oil. It took hours, and a Herculean effort, to mix it back to something that resembled creamy, but once done, it was pretty damn good.

I'm not sure if it was a bet or a dare from one of my brothers, or just me being stupidly curious, but I was convinced the oil sitting on top was where the peanut flavor came from. One day when a fresh can was just opened I grabbed a spoon and scooped up some of the oil and, without hesitation, ate it in one gulp.

I'm pretty sure I vomited.

The taste had an underlying harsh feel, or maybe it was just the shock that it didn't taste anything like the peanut butter I was used to. It was like the time I bit into a bar of unsweetened bakers' chocolate and my taste buds screamed in revolt.

The oily texture and raw taste have haunted me my entire life.

This was Hill Street, a place where the poor people lived. We, on the other hand, didn't know any better. We did have friends that lived on other streets, lived in "real" houses, but for the most part, we all kept pretty much to ourselves. We were close friends: we dated each other, had babies together, and even in some cases married each other. Race, color, religion-- none of it mattered because we were all the same poor.

It's the type of place that seems to embed itself into your DNA. Even decades later, all it takes is to have "Freebird" blast out of the car speakers and you're drifting back to the funky free lunches at the summer playground that seemed to be mostly green bologna and warm apple juice; the tick-infested grass forts we made after they cut the back field; or just hanging in the parking lot doing things you really don't want to admit to, but still smile about.

It has taken middle age for me to realize that the street reflects who I am, some good some bad, but all me.

STORIES FROM THE STREET

I

It was summer of 1971, I think, and three bored ten-year-olds were walking around looking for something to do.

With me was Craig who lived at the end of my unit. He had that classic Italian American look that John Travolta would make famous in a couple years, and although all the girls thought he was cute, I don't think he really knew or understood that, which made him even more desirable to the girls.

There was also James, a real good friend for the short time he lived across the yard from me. He had this mane of shoulder-length red hair that framed a long, serious face. I always thought he would make a great front man for a rock band. He also had a "let's do it and worry later" attitude, the perfect mind for mischief.

His parents made for an odd couple: his dad was a hot shit named Buck who was beer drinking buddies with my Dad, was quick with a joke, and even quicker with a backhand if you needed it. James's mom was a tad scary; she sold Avon products and would knock on your door at all hours of the night, especially if you owed her money.

Once again, the architect of the plan is lost to a lifetime of dead brain cells, but it was simple enough: we were going to "creep" a house party that was going on, and hopefully sneak away with some free beer.

John and Joe were two brothers who were the closest experience for me of hippies. I'm not sure they would fit the true definition of hippies, but in my world, they were young, carefree, and gentle souls. They were friendly to a fault, and except for the random parties, they didn't bother anyone. Somehow, John and Joe convinced the Housing Authority to let them continue living in the unit after their mom died, which was an achievement in itself.

Two young guys, popular and liked to party, with a place of their own. What could possibly go wrong?

Our plan was for me to look into the open living-room window, and Craig and James would wait by the back door. Once I gave the all-clear signal, Craig and

James were to sneak in through the back door, and Craig would be the lookout as James grabbed some beer. That was the plan, anyway.

I grabbed the window ledge and pulled myself up on my tippy-toes, and at first all I could see was a dozen or so people jammed into the small room. The music was loud and there was a dense cloud of smoke hanging above everyone's heads. I was trying to see through the bodies into the doorway to the kitchen so I could signal when little to no people were in there, but my view was blocked.

Move, people, move, I wished, and as if they all heard me the wall of bodies split to each side of the room giving me a clear view of a girl dancing by the stairs.

My eyes blew open as wide as humanly possible, my heart began racing, and I just may have forgotten how to breathe for a moment. She was tall and thin, with shiny black hair that went to the middle of her back, and she had on a pair of very sheer white panties, so sheer she might as well have been naked, and she wore nothing else.

She was facing the window, her arms swinging at her side, her body and head tilted back and eyes closed, swaying back and forth to the music. Of course, my eyes focused on her boobs. They were small, what us cavemen would call a handful, perky and jiggling just enough to make me flushed and on the verge of fainting. I couldn't believe no one else was paying attention to her.

In a blink I was tossed to the ground, and at first, I thought someone caught me, but I saw Craig and James both with their heads in the window.

I guess our plans had now changed.

We didn't sneak any beer that night, but I got to see my first naked girl. Well, she was naked enough.

I got to know both John and Joe over the years, and the sad thing is they probably would have given us a beer of two if we'd asked.

But what fun would that have been?

II

My cousin Jimmy was considered the seventh Barry. He was always around; he was there for morning coffee, he was there for the cookouts, and he was there for a lot of meals. As all of us grew older, Jimmy was part of the card nights, game nights, couples nights, and never missed a party. He had a wide, infectious smile and a deep, recognizable laugh. When you heard it, you knew right away it came from Jimmy.

My wife and I rented a place down by the water for a couple of weeks, and on the second day we were walking up from the beach and noticed an old, beat-up vehicle parked in front of the cottage. I was pissed at first, thinking some asshole parked there and went off to the beach, but as we got closer, I saw Jimmy come out of the cottage and retrieve a cooler out of the car.

"Hey!" I yelled, both relieved and pleased it was him. "How long you staying?"

"How long you have the cottage?" he answered.

He was never a big guy; however, in later years he did develop what became known as the Barry Beer Belly. In his younger years though, he was fit, and a bit of a sportsman. Surprising, considering his Sunday routine.

Jimmy was part of the Sunday morning coffee drinkers at my house. I'm not sure he came for the coffee as much as he did for a chance to help Dad prep for Sunday dinner. Dad's Sunday cooking is what inspired my love of cooking, and I like to think it may have inspired Jimmy as well. As an adult, Jimmy grew into a good caterer.

Then again, the inspiration may have been for an extra meal.

In our household Monday through Saturday, the main meal was held around five in the evening and was called "supper." On Sunday, the main meal was held at noon and called "dinner." I'm not sure why-- it was like that my entire life-- and although the Sunday dinner tradition struggles but is still alive, none of us eat at noon anymore. Even during football season, we will eat at half-time, which is closer to three.

I always thought it had something to do with Dad working all week, doing the shopping on Saturday, and cooking on Sunday. If he served us early, he had the rest of the afternoon to just chill out. Maybe, just maybe it had some deep, historical meaning involving the grandmother who raised him, but I think he just wanted a couple hours of rest after a good meal.

On many a Sunday as we sat down at noon for the meal, Jimmy would join us. While he was eating at our house, my Aunt, his mom, was next door cooking their Sunday meal which she served around two. By the time Jimmy's first dinner was settling in his stomach, his mom was setting the table, and Jimmy was right there sitting at his spot with fork in hand.

With what must have been a stomach-exploding amount of food in his belly, Jimmy would hobble across the street to his girlfriend's house. This family had dinner around five, and Jimmy would say they would hand him a plate, and he didn't want to insult anyone, but I believe he was willing and able to force a third meal down.

This wasn't every week, but more often than not this was the Sunday dinner schedule of Jimmy.

III

The first truck always seemed to come early afternoon, not long after lunch time. A white box of a thing, but smaller than the other truck that competed for us poor kids' pocket change.

The truck came complete with pictures of icy treats plastered around the serving window like some postal truck lost inside a Candy Land board game.

It also had an annoying buzzer that if you were close enough, you could feel it in the roots of your teeth. If that wasn't enough to get your attention, it also had a bullhorn-like speaker on the roof that poured out the worst of the worst for a 70s inner city kid: old, knee-slapping country music.

This was the truck that sold the hard ice cream: the popsicles, Fudgsicles, and basically anything frozen on a stick.

This was also one of those hard choices in life they tell you about. The ones that at the time seem not to mean much, but end up being a strand in the spiderweb that becomes your life, and all that bullshit. It was a choice that became even more important if you had limited funds: do I buy now, or do I wait for the other guy?

As you can already guess I usually made the wrong choice.

Those smarter than me would wait, but my willpower and self-esteem are very low when it comes to ice cream. It didn't matter how little pocket change I had, or how early the first truck came: at the first sight of it turning down the street, when that tinny music and eye-squinting buzzer hit my ears, I would cave.

More often than not I would end up with the "Bomb Pop." Not really ice cream at all, but a glacier-sized hunk of ice in the shape of a futuristic rocket ship, colored in red, white, and blue layers. The sheer size of the thing would make you think it would last the better part of the summer, but it always seemed that the faster you licked, the faster it melted, and for the rest of the day both my lips and shirt would be stained like some bizarre American flag.

To add insult to injury, in the late afternoon, timed almost perfectly after dinner, you would hear the circus-like music growing louder as the white-and-blue UPS-sized truck drove down the street. This was the Mr. Softy truck. He had the soft-serve stuff: no wanted posters of frozen icebergs here. Painted on both sides of the truck was a giant smiley faced soft-serve cone with hair that was a swirl of vanilla ice cream, and a blue coat and bow tie at the bottom of the cone.

He only had three options: vanilla, chocolate and-- insert the heavens opening and angels singing-- the vanilla-chocolate swirl.

Everyone always crowded around the serving window, watching in chin-dropped awe at the spotless stainless-steel machines and the Mr. Softy guy who would pull up on one of the three levers, and with deft hands, swirl the ice cream into the cone. The only fly in this near-perfect ice cream dream was that to me, the cone itself always tasted like a sweeter version of the communion wafer they gave you at church.

What Mr. Softy lacked in variety, he more than made up for in toppings. I was always blown away as the Mr. Softy guy dipped the cone upside down into the hot strawberry or chocolate sauce that set instantly to a candy coating, or like a magician's sleight of hand, he would spread colored sprinkles, chocolate crunch, or my favorite, the butter crunch, over the ice cream without incident. We watched and wondered how he could do all that when we couldn't walk in a straight line without dropping, or dripping, the cone all over the place.

Just a pure, forgotten work of art.

No matter what size you got, or better yet, were able to afford, the soft-serve seemed to at first defy gravity. You learned early to keep your arm stiff, but bent at the elbow at about 45 degrees, and for some reason if you looked directly at the teetering swirl of ice cream, it somehow helped your balance so you could make it to a spot to sit down before it toppled over or melted.

Still, you had a one-in-ten chance of the ice cream falling to the ground as you made your way back across the street. The *splat!* as the cone hit the pavement like a report from a gun would turn all heads in shocked horror that soon turned to guilt as everyone huddled closer around their own cones. Those whom you thought were your friends crept faster away from you, not wanting to experience the same fate, and not wanting to share.

Sometimes, if you were close enough to the truck to be seen, the Mr. Softy guy would have a bit of mercy and replace your cone. Then again, you could be like me, standing on the far side of the street with stained lips and stained shirt, wishing, once again, you had waited just a couple more hours.

I'm guessing I was 8 or 9, and up to that point, birthdays were really no big deal. I really don't have any memory of birthday parties, although I remember seeing a picture of Buddy sitting at the kitchen table with a cake in front of him, and some houses made out of Legos surrounding it. I do remember those Legos; I wasn't allowed to play with them often, but when I could, I would spend hours on them. My guess is this was just family and cake for what looks like Buddy's birthday. Strangely enough, his birthday is just two weeks after mine.

On this particular birthday, Dad was on his way to a Fraternal Order of Eagles meeting, and he told me he gave my mother money to get cake and ice cream. I remember my disappointment when he said he wouldn't be home for the cake, but he gave me a couple of dollars for the store.

I was on my way to the store when I spotted my brother Joey getting into the driver's side of a car. He didn't own a car so it caught my attention right away. I ran over as he was starting the car up.

"Hey Joey, where you'd get the car? Where ya going?" I asked. I'm not really sure why I was so excited.

"It's Cindy's mom's car," he told me, and I noticed his girlfriend, now wife, Cindy, sitting beside him. "We're going to the movies."

"Can I go? Dad gave me two dollars." I remember hopping from one foot to the other, waiting for an answer.

"No." Short, blunt, and the car was moving away from the curb.

It was hard enough being shot down so harshly, but as I stood there with the dollar bills crumpled in my hand, the harshness changed to crushing. As the car began picking up speed, bouncing down the street, two heads bobbed up into the back window. Two blonde, giggly, girly heads smiled at me as the car reached the corner and turned out of sight. Cindy's sisters, both younger than me, were in the back seat.

Feeling hurt, the two dollars forgotten but still clenched in my hand, I forgot all about the store and headed home.

I could smell chocolate baking as soon as I entered the courtyard, and normally I wouldn't even think of my house, but it was my birthday. I felt like that cartoon where the character is whisked off their feet by smokey fingers of aroma, magically lifting them away to the cooling pie sitting in a window sill. Only in my case, it was chocolate cake.

Bursting through the back door into the kitchen, I saw the cake was in fact a tray of brownies my mother had baked. Only the tray was now empty except for some crumbs and a heavy aroma mocking me.

No cake, no ice cream, no candles, no family and friends gathering to sing happy birthday. Just a glass serving tray with the remains of some brownies.

I ended up sitting against the end of my building, crying. Two young black girls, sisters who lived with their mom in one of the apartments across the courtyard, appeared and asked why I was crying. Maybe it was their warm smiles, genuine concern, their honest compassion, or maybe I was just starved for any affection, but without effort or ability to stop it, the events of the day spilled out of my mouth.

I think I may have embarrassed myself because I ran home, a new burst of tears streaking my face, and I hid in the bathroom until my mother banged on the door for me to get out.

Hours later the two girls were at my back door; they said their mom wanted to see me. My suspicions were up, but the girls were smiling-- no, they were beaming-- and grabbing my hand before I could say no. They dragged me across the courtyard.

It bothers me I don't remember their names, but when I walked into their kitchen, the lights went out and their mother held out a chocolate cake with flaming candles. They sang happy birthday and pushed the cake closer for me to blow the candles out.

I think I cried again.

For my brother Joey, don't worry. My obsession with celebrations had nothing to do with you taking your girlfriend's sisters to the movies. It came from a mom and her two daughters who in that brief, innocent moment told me I matter.

Like an addict, I have been searching ever since to feel again what I felt that day in their kitchen.

THE BEST CHIPS EVER

I was 13.

It was one of those Friday nights with no one around, nowhere to go and nothing to do. I was good with that, though. I was comfortable with my own company, and unlike most of the kids I hung with, I didn't mind the occasional off day. I was already a heavy reader and I was already dabbling in writing to occupy my time.

good or bad, I have Dad to thank for that.

I remember the mornings going down to the kitchen before the coffee crowd arrived and finding Dad, unfiltered Pall Mall cigarette between his fingers and the first cup of coffee in front of him, reading an old western or 'Dime Store' mystery book. As a result, reading became our common-thread, our topic for conversations and the one thing with Dad I didn't have to compete with my brothers over.

In Seventh grade he gave me a book that became the gateway to the literary addiction I have today. The book was 'The Red Badge of Courage'.

On this particular Friday night, it was neither the reading or the writing that excited me, it was a back to back feature of horror movies scheduled on channel 56. This was a local station out of Boston that aired all my favorite morning cartoons, all the off-beat sitcoms I loved, and was not afraid to run the worst of the 50's and 60's horror films that freaks like me watched.

Again, I put the blame of my love of old movies on Dad.

There are far too many memories of he and I watching wrestling on Saturday afternoon while we ate a dinner of hotdog, beans, sauerkraut and brown bread from a can. The normal Saturday meal. There were also lazy Sunday afternoons filled with old black and white war movies, and reruns of old westerns. Even today I think of him when I come across an old black and white, my wife and kids roll their eyes as I sit there with a dumb ass smile on my face, and they don't understand why.

The low-grade horror, on the other hand, is all me.

Dad turned this night into an event by telling me he was going out and I could use the television in his room, he then gave me a dollar for snacks.

A room to myself, a television to myself and snacks to myself. Heaven couldn't even be as good as this.

After some painful negotiations with my brain at the store I decided on a bag of sour cream and onion potato chips and a bottle of cola. I left the store with a face full of smile, a bag full of snacks and even a pocket full of change that was left over. All I knew it was good to be me that night, and I strutted towards home.

The trip took me into the back field and behind the Teen Center. I could see glowing blue spilling out of the windows from the black-lights, and the walls were vibrating with loud heavy metal music. The older teens were having a dance, and they owned the center now. It was not a place I would be welcomed.

"Johnny!" It was my cousin Mikey sitting on the Teen Center back step.

Mikey was my Aunts middle child, and as the middle child was as different from his brothers as I was from mine. Unlike them he wasn't good at sports, I never saw him in a fight and he had a laidback almost carefree way of looking at things. More importantly his was the only one of Auntie's kids that had the Barry look about him; He was tall like most of the Barry's, except me, and had that Barry whole face smile that was infectious.

We became friends in later years, but he was a few years older than me and on that night we were just cousin's.

"Come here!" He said.

I saw next to him was his best friend Susan. I don't think they ever really became boyfriend and girlfriend, but they were always together. They went to school together, to parties together, hung out together and saying the words Mikey and Susan became as common as saying Mom and Dad.

They may never have been boyfriend and girlfriend, but I've always known them to be best friends.

I walked over towards them without thinking. Mikey was not mean, was not a bully, he may have been a jokester and enjoyed a good prank now and then, but there was nothing cruel about him.

"What's up, Mikey?" I was about to ask, but before the words came out Susan had grabbed my bag of snacks and Mikey tackled me to the ground, pinning my arms down with his knees. I saw a home-rolled joint between the index finger and thumb of his right hand, and I could smell the sweet, earthy smell of pot coming from the glowing red tip.

Before I could resist Mikey put the lit end of the joint into his mouth, leaned down to within a couple inches of my face and blew out. My face was quickly encased in smoke, and Mikey's weight pressing down on me caused me to breath in deep, filling my lungs. I felt a burning wave in my chest and a spasm of coughing erupted. A minute later as the coughing began to subside Mikey blew another cloud into my face. Once again, my lungs drew in more of the smoke then I wanted and another coughing spasm began, not as bad as the first. Mikey waited until I calmed down and blew a third cloud into my face and climbed off me.

As I rolled over coughing, I could hear both of them laughing, but it sounded as if the laughter was coming from the back of a tunnel. I stood up and found my bag back in my hand, not knowing how it got there, and as I started walking again Mikey and Susan headed towards the entrance to the center.

The walk home was slower, my legs felt almost rubbery, and I couldn't help but look in every direction at everything and at nothing all at the same time. It seemed like hours to get home, although it was more like twenty minutes, and I was scared, at first, to go inside. I didn't know why.

I felt like a zombie as I walked into the back door. Billy was in the living room watching television, I didn't know where Mom was, or if she was even home. I fought to look normal, which only made me look weirder, and climbed the stairs as quickly as I could.

I didn't calm down until I was in Dad's room, television on, and the bag of chips opened.

It was a few years later that I understood why the horror film I've seen a dozen times was extra scary that night. By the end of the second movie I was convinced someone was living in my father's closet.

It was also the best chips I've ever ate.

LET IT BURN LIKE THE FOURTH OF JULY

BLITZ

Angry skies exploding
In great flashes of light.
There is confusion,
Disillusion,
The foul stench of burning flesh.
You pray,
You cry,
You scream,
You die.

BONFIRE

I

The fire trucks were now gone.

Someone had tipped off the fire department, and just before dusk they arrived in force. One truck came onto the field through the gates by the Housing Authority Maintenance Building, one was on the side street directly behind the baseball field backstop, and one was standing by on the street.

A team of firefighters, fire hoses in hand, stood in front of the backstop, now covered by a towering pile of junk and old furniture dripping in gasoline. A second firefighting team came at the pile from the woods behind the backstop, and with a hand motion from a man who looked very annoyed to be there, both teams opened their nozzles and began soaking down the pile before it was ever kissed by the fire.

It was an hour before the firefighters were packed up and gone, and in their wake was a water-logged pile of trash. Now useless, it looked to be the first time in over a decade there would be no Fourth of July bonfire in the Hill Street field.

Or so we thought.

His name was Allen, a young black teen from the street, and as the disappointed crowd began to leave, Allen made his way to the field with another can of gas. He climbed the back of the 20-foot-high backstop fence, and with the last of the day's light peeking over the horizon, he poured the gas over the top of the water-drenched and dripping debris. It was maybe a couple of gallons' worth, and nobody thought it would make a difference, but Allen didn't seem to care: he was determined, and with one leg slung over the top of the fence to brace himself, he poured out the last of the can.

At first, I thought it was a firefly, a small speck of light lobbing across the sky towards the pile. It had a sparkle to it, a sizzle-like look as it landed somewhere in the center of the mess. Somewhere in the back of my brain I realized it was not a firefly but a firecracker, a small, simple firecracker, and most of the crowd didn't even notice the dull, uneventful *pop* causing a chain reaction.

It was more of a *whoomph* than an explosion. Kind of like when the heat kicks on, but a thousand times louder. A small, yellow ball grew from the center of the heap, and within seconds raced out and up the pile, consuming all in its path. The flames punched a funnel of hot air upwards, and before Allen could react, the punch hit him full force, knocking him from his perch and sending him 20 feet to the ground.

The crowd gave a collective gasp as the fireball settled into a large, steady fire, many forgetting anyone was even on the fence. A handful rushed to the back of the fire expecting the worst, and finding Allen on his back in the grass, shook-up but smiling, and proud of single-handedly saving the tradition.

In reality, it was more logistics than Allen's small can of gas: the stacking of pallets, couches, and old tables created a number of air pockets, and the gas filled these pockets with very flammable fumes. The couple of gallons Allen used helped, but it was the sheer amount of gas poured on the pile while it was being built that was the main source of ignition. So much gas was used that even the fire department's soaking was not enough to dilute it, and the gallons of water probably helped seal those air pockets, condensing the fumes.

All it took was some idiot with a tiny firecracker and Fate's hand tumbling that firecracker in the air to land at the exact spot where a fume-filled air pocket was.

Pop, *whoomph*, awe.

Regardless of the science behind it, Allen still holds center stage for the most memorable bonfire.

II

One of the things the developers got right was they left half of the street's property undeveloped; a section was set aside with shade trees and playground equipment, and another section was asphalted over and turned into a basketball court. The court had a six-inch lip around it, and Mark Federico discovered how to flood this in the winter to ice skate on. They also left a grassy strip running the length of the street that included a makeshift baseball diamond.

The baseball field wasn't much-- we had to use coats and t-shirts as bases, and would make the baselines out of anything white we could find-- but for kids that couldn't afford the signup fees for Little League, it was good enough.

Even the Hill Street moms got involved with the field. One summer a group of teachers created a couple of softball teams, and in the early afternoons would take over the baseball field for their games. The moms took offense that the teachers, without asking, took the field away from the kids and mounted their own protest.

For most of the week when the teachers arrived, they found the moms sitting on the bases, pitcher's mound, and home base, refusing to move. If I'm not mistaken, the teachers came back with a permit, but the moms still would not move. I do believe the police arrived at some point, but what are you supposed to do with a dozen women who live on the street refusing to move off the field so people who don't live on the street can take the field away from the kids?

The protest was simple: the kids spent a lot of time and effort making the field usable, and did such a good job that these teachers took the field over for their own use. The moms didn't think it was fair, and their protest worked: the teachers eventually gave up and stopped coming to the field.

The annual bonfire planning began as early as May, timed around tax returns. This is back before the ability to submit income taxes online to get your return check in a couple weeks; we had to snail-mail everything and wait 6 to 8 weeks.

As the kids say today, "The struggle was real."

The connection between the bonfire and tax returns is that was the only time any of us could afford to buy anything big. If you needed a new table, new couch, or any larger ticket item, this was the time to purchase it. The old bed or kitchen table was stored until the Fourth of July.

It didn't take long for both the police and Housing Authority to catch on to the collecting of big items. Throughout June, a dump truck and half a dozen city workers would ride up and down the street collecting anything of bulk to haul off to the dump, the theory being that if there was nothing to burn, then there would be no annual bonfire.

Hill Streeters were a step ahead; each two units shared a finished basement space, although we northerners called it "the cellar." By finished, I mean it had a cement floor and walls and was just better than a crawl space, not more than 4 feet tall.

The space was mainly for maintenance guys to have access to pipes and electric wires, but we used it for storage as well. There was a bulkhead and stairs in between every other unit, and through laziness, not giving a shit, or just plain stupidity, the Housing Authority never checked the cellars.

That POS particle board entertainment center that fell apart right after Christmas? Shove it in the cellar.

That mattress that little Timmy peed on all winter? Shove it in the cellar.

Those god-awful red seats you yanked out of your newly painted black '69 Nova? Toss them in a cellar.

The cat-clawed couch you just replaced with your income tax return? It goes in the cellar.

There were a hundred families on the street, and most donated something to the cause. It made for a pretty decent bonfire.

It depended on what decade you lived in as to what the procedures were. In the 60s just before sunset, the bulkhead doors would swing open and spit out their stored merchandise. Not unlike an army of worker ants, groups of kids would carry everything across the field and to the backstop. The designated organizer would supervise the piling up, making sure the pile was high and tight for a better burn.

Between 9 and 10 p.m. cans of gas, most siphoned from unsuspecting neighbors on other streets, would be tossed on the pile, and a match would ignite it. In just under an hour, the police and fire would arrive, the firetruck using the gated path by the maintenance building to gain access to the field and wait for the fire to reach its peak. When red sparks drifted to the woods, they would open the nozzles of the hoses and put the fire down.

The total time of the fire, at best, was 90 minutes.

In the 70s there was still enough debris stored in the cellars, but this was also supplemented by picnic tables, small sheds, and anything burnable that neighboring streets left unattended. One year the entire stock of building material from a construction site on the street behind us found its way to the pile.

This generation also spent as much time preventing police and fire from getting on the field as they did building the bonfire. During one most creative year, spikes were hammered through sheets of plywood, which were then laid out at the entrance of the field, spike-side up. In back of the backstop, the paths in the woods were lined with pallets to block, or hinder, any attack from behind.

As night fell, and we were all well-stocked with pot and beer, the fire began. The sheets of spiked plywood worked for a moment or two-- police were able to quickly move the plywood out of the way-- and we misjudged the power of water coming out of a high-pressure hose; firefighters were able to hit the bonfire without having to come down any of the paths.

It was all a learning experience; one year we chained and padlocked the entrance to the field, never thinking that firefighters had bolt cutters.

The total time of the fire was maybe an hour.

The 80s brought a diminished interest in the tradition. The fires were smaller, the crowds more aggressive, and the public safety net fell earlier and tighter around the street during the Fourth of July. Very few were left who collected burnable stuff, and it seemed the street increasingly became more interested that their 9mm was locked and loaded than if there was a bonfire at all.

This was around the time I moved off the street, and I'm not sad about that.

The average time of fire, if it happened at all, was less than half an hour.

What also occurs to me is that in the thirty years of the Hill Street Fourth of July bonfires, I don't think there was any year the fire was allowed to burn down. I don't think anyone has ever seen a Hill Street bonfire burn from start to finish.

III

It had the feel of an outdoor concert about to go wrong.

There was a good hundred people in the back field, most squeezed into the baseball diamond in front of the pile of debris that was ready to burn. Amongst the crowd were a number of kids from the area we called 'Indian Heights', a development of single-family ranch houses located behind the middle school across the street from us.

The kids from Indian Heights were financially better off then us, wore better clothes than us, and in general thought they were better than us. This particular summer they decided they deserved our back field as their personal hangout, because they were better and they were entitled.

"They are encroaching on our turf," the Hollywood screenwriter would say.

The tensions between us were already growing by the time Fourth of July came around. It didn't help that they felt entitled to our bonfire as well, and as dusk rolled around, there were a good dozen or so Indian Heights crew pushing their way to the front of the crowd.

Not that the bonfire was going to be any big deal; its size and excitement had been dwindling over the years, and this year the pile was no higher than 10 feet at best. Almost all of the debris had been stolen from backyards of homes bordering Hill Street.

Regardless, a fire is a fire, and I had my spot, a six pack of beer, and a dozen home-rolled joints in a cigarette pack in my pocket. I was going to enjoy the fire no matter how small, or how long it lasted.

In the blink of an eye, it all changed.

95

An Indian Heights kid, well on his way to being drunk, and probably stoned, bumped his shoulder into mine as he walked by.

"Excuse you," I said.

"What?" he turned around.

"You fucking bumped into me, asshole."

"Fuck you."

"No, fuck you." We were nose to nose.

There is a stage in any argument that you know is the point of no return, and there is going to be a fight. This kid may not have figured it out, but I knew punches were about to be thrown.

Behind me someone, and I'm not sure who, was tugging on the back of my shirt, talking into my ear. "Hit him, Johnny, hit him," the voice said.

I slowly brought my right arm back, clenching my fist. When I saw the arrogant little bastard blink, I swung my arm forward, full force, aiming for the side of his head, and at the point of contact, my fist kept going, the force of my fist finding nothing but air spinning me around. The kid was gone.

Unbeknownst to me, my brother Buddy had shown up as I was ready to swing. He mistook the tugging on my shoulder as this kid punching me and jumped in to help his little brother. He grabbed the kid by his shirt and swung him through the air. None of us saw the police cruiser arrive until the kid landed on the hood.

The police knew this wasn't going to end well for this kid, and he was hustled into the back of the cruiser.

"I'm going to get you!" he yelled from the back seat to my brother.

I should have felt honored and proud that my brother would come to my rescue like that, and I was and still am, but on that night I was pissed. He stole my fight away from me, a point that to this day, I remind him of.

The crowd broke up pretty fast after that, and normally it would have been the end of it except this kid with a belly full of liquid courage, inside the safety of a police cruiser, yelled a threat to my brother.

"You can't let that go," Buddy explained to me, "you can't spend your life looking over your shoulder thinking this guy is going come after you." I got it, understood fully. Buddy was married with kids at this point and couldn't chance some nut-job chasing after him.

The word went out that my brother was looking for this kid, and I was surprised the kid showed up in the field with some of his friends a couple days later. Buddy was at his mothers-in-law's house on the other end of the street, and it started with just he and I walking towards the field, but word traveled fast and by time we came into view of the kid and his friends, there were over a dozen people walking with us.

The sight of a dozen "scary" project kids must have freaked out his friends, because they immediately jumped into their cars and sped off, leaving their friend alone.

I have to give this kid credit; he stood his ground, showed no fear, and walked up to my brother and I and apologized to both of us. He said he was drunk and didn't mean to be an asshole. He then shook both our hands, ending the last Hill Street bonfire experience for me.

RANDOM SHIT

TWISTED FATE

A twisted fate
For you and me.
To see the magic
Within your eyes.
To hear the wisp
Of your golden hair.
To smell the breeze
As you walk by.
To know this love
Will never be.
Such a twisted fate
For you and me.

ON THE STAIRS SHE WAITED

I was still in elementary school, no more than fifth grade, and my brother had a new girlfriend. It was young love, straight out of a Hollywood movie set, and the two of them were short-circuiting over the bliss they thought would last forever. Of course, they wanted to share this with anyone and everyone.

The girlfriend had a sister who was my age, and couldn't resist, and she and my brother came up with this idea to get me and the sister together. Their love-fogged minds hatched the plan that started with sitting the sister down and convincing her I was coming over the house the following morning to walk her to school.

The following morning, the sister waited on the front steps.

Years later, married with three children and a mortgage, I was either with my brother at a bar, or in his backyard in front of the fire talking about old times. For whatever reason he remembered the plot to get his girlfriend's sister and I together, and how they told her I would walk her to school.

The problem with this plan was they forgot to tell me.

This girl waited on the steps and I never showed up.

I was horrified. Throughout the years I crossed paths with this girl, never realizing I stood her up. Never realizing we had what at our age would have been considered a date. Never realizing I unknowingly hurt her feelings.

Maybe that's why this keeps poking its head out; I guess you could say I had a crush on her from time to time, and maybe my brain keeps asking what if.

IT'S A SHAME HE BEATS HER

The following is a phone conversation between my mother and my wife's grandmother as it was told to me. This took place not long after Debby and I began dating, but I didn't find out until years later.

Kay: *Hello, is this Debby's grandmother?*

Estelle: *Yes, it is, who is this?*

Kay: *This is Johnny's mother, Kay.*

Estelle: *Hello Kay, nice to speak to you. I'm Estelle.*

Kay: *I just wanted to tell you what a wonderful person Debby is.*

Estelle: *Thank you, yes, she is a wonderful person.*

Kay: *I'm so glad Johnny finally found someone. Debby is so good for him, it's a shame he beats her.*

Estelle: *(silence)*

Estelle calls her granddaughter as soon as she hangs up from Kay. Debby lives with Estelle, they see each other every day, they talk every day, so she wasn't overly concerned. Yet, she is very protective of the girl she played a major role in raising, and there has to be a reason why a mother would say something like that about their son.

It was a number of years before Estelle and I were comfortable with each other. I had the impression she never fully trusted me, and always wrote it off as nobody would be good enough for her Debby-Doo.

Deb and I were married by a Justice of the Peace, and the plan was to have a family dinner afterwards at the restaurant where Estelle hosted. Estelle drove us to and from the simple ceremony, and on the way to the restaurant she pulled the car over, turned to look me in the eye and said, "Welcome to the family, but if you hurt my Debby in any way, I will shoot your balls off."

I now wonder if that phone call from my mother played any part in Estelle and I's strained relationship.

I have never discovered why my mother said that to my girlfriend's grandmother that day. I can proudly say I have never hit a woman, in anger or otherwise, in my life.

THE GIRL AND THE FAT KID

I was barely old enough to have a crush, but still young enough for the event to create a deep emotional scar.

She had an oval face that still held onto some of her pre-teen chubbiness, perfectly framed by straight, shoulder-length chestnut hair. When she smiled, which she did often, her cheeks dimpled, and I was in awe of her bright white teeth. Of course, she was out of my league, but I liked her and couldn't help myself.

We were sitting on the cement steps in front of her apartment, just the two of us. Surprisingly, I felt at ease talking about anything and nothing with her. I was feeling good that I was making her laugh, a lot, and at one point our hands moved and touched, and she didn't move her hand away. I found myself lost within her brown eyes, not hearing anything except a crackly voice yelling from the street.

"Get your fat ass over here and help me with these bags!" It was my mother, standing in front of the open trunk of a taxi cab.

The moment was lost, her hands now on her lap, and her smile gone. I stood up and walked towards the street, but I guess not fast enough.

"What are you doing?" my mother yelled loud enough for the girl to hear. "Girls don't like fat kids."

I avoided that girl as much as people who live on the same street can. From that point on we would say hello in passing, but not much more.

SCHOOL DAZE

When you're teaching someone what you know, never teach them all you know. That's real job security.

-Words of wisdom from Dad

NAILS, NUNS, AND NURSES

I was nine years old.

I was late for school.

I thought the path cutting through the small patch of woods would be quicker.

I'm not sure what my older brothers dealt with, but by the time the stork dropped me into the fray, Mom was in no mood to get up early to get us off to school. When it came to getting up, washing up, having any semblance of a breakfast, and making a lunch, those chores were all on us. All of which, at nine, was tough enough without the added wrinkle of being late.

I don't know if I fell back to sleep, or never woke up in the first place. When my internal clock finally snapped my eyes awake, the house was quiet, my brothers were gone, and the arms on the alarm clock were pointing to 8:15. The late bell for school was 8:05, and school was a good 20-minute hustle away.

The shortest distance between two spots is a straight line, and that straight line took me through the back field, across the street behind us, and into the woods on the other side of that street. It was really nothing more than a dense patch of trees and brush with a dirt path that snaked to the other street, but it cut your time to school by half.

On any other day the path wouldn't have bothered me-- most mornings there were a dozen or so kids going in the same direction-- but that morning, I was alone.

The fear of facing Sister Mary Finbarr, the principal of the school, kept my mind focused on my steady jog forward so I didn't even notice the other kid standing just inside the brush until he stepped back onto the path.

"What's your name?" he asked. His voice slow, forced, almost angry. The red flags in my brain began waving frantically, and the pit in my stomach clenched up like a fist.

I guessed his age at 16, maybe 17, and he was dressed in an oversized dungaree jacket that was faded, dirty, and frayed at the elbows. His pants, also dungaree, looked newer-- a darker blue-- and the legs were rolled up with what looked like a four-inch cuff. I don't remember much of his face; he had a rats-nest uncombed head of blonde hair that strung down to his shoulders, but that was all my mind saw. My attention was fully focused on the board he held in his hands.

It was as long and twice as thick as a yardstick, and had that grayish look of an aged piece of wooden fence. He was holding it like a bat; his right hand gripped the bottom and was swinging it up and down into the palm of his left hand.

I knew if I answered him my voice would give away the fear that was bubbling up from my stomach. I was frozen in place, horrified but trying hard to make it look like I was standing my ground.

"Pull your pants down or I'll hit you with this," he sneered, slapping the board harder into his hand.

I looked past him, seeing the house at the end of the path, a woman walking down the driveway with a trash can. I wanted to yell, wanted to scream for help, but I couldn't. I was a Barry, I was from the Hill Street Projects, I had tough older brothers and an even tougher father. There was no calling for help, and I did the only thing my brain could come up with to do.

"Fuck you!" I yelled, my voice breaking, my eyes flooding over.

My tear-filled vision saw the kid swing the board downward toward my legs and I jumped as high as I could.

I wasn't fast enough.

The nail sticking out of the end of the board easily passed through the jeans of my left leg and into the meat of my calf. The fabric of my pants kept the nail head from poking into my skin no more than an eighth of an inch or so, but it was still enough to make it bleed and cause a white, blinding pain to shoot across my eyes.

As my feet landed back onto solid ground, the board was pulled up. A new blinding pain raced across my brain as the nail tore a two-inch gap into my leg, releasing a new trail of blood.

Although I was blinded by fear and pain, the fight or flight still kicked in; I was too young and too small to fight so I forced my legs to move, and the last vision I had of him was the board held in a batting position as he was about to swing again.

It was a ten-minute run to the schoolyard and I didn't look back until I had the school in sight. My heart was pounding, my lungs burning, but nobody was following me.

My leg was throbbing, and my eyes were still leaking, but I was holding it together as much as possible. As I walked up the cement stairs and into the main door of Saint Colman's Elementary School, I was starting to feel it was going to be OK. As I stepped into the main hall, Sister Mary Finbarr was there to greet me.

"Are we just getting in, Mr. Barry?" she asked, her voice slow, steady, and echoing around the inside of my ears as if God himself were speaking.

She did not have a kind face. The headpiece of her habit only enhanced the deep creases on her forehead, around her eyes, and the edges of her mouth so she always had a displeased look about her. It didn't matter if she was happy, sad, or actually displeased; it was always the same. I never saw her change her expression. As head disciplinarian it may have worked, but for a child in need of some emotional help, it just added to the fear.

I looked up at her stern face, put on the bravest front I could muster, and opened my mouth to speak-- that was when it all crashed down. The words got lost, and all that came out was a deep moan as my eyes lost their battle of holding back tears, and they came rushing out to race down my cheeks. It was then, I think, she noticed the wet, red stain surrounding the ripped fabric on my leg.

An hour later I was in my gym shorts laying on the cot in the nurse's office. I had a wet, folded washcloth on my forehead and a fist-sized bandage on my leg. I guess the nurse had a recent tetanus shot on file and the wound did not need stitches, so a trip to the hospital was not needed. The nurse gave me some aspirin, cleaned the wound, and closed it using a few small Band-Aids. It hurt like hell, but I clamped my jaws down and took it; I needed to make up for the breakdown in the hallway.

The school did call the police in, they questioned me, I answered as best I could, and they said they would get back in touch if they found the guy. They never did.

The nurse tried all day to get in touch with my mother; she never answered the phone, and by the time school was letting out, I convinced the nurse it would be ok for me to walk home with my friends. I'm sure she had reservations, but also no choice but to let me go. She found a baggy pair of sweatpants for me to wear, put my blood-stained paints in a bag with a letter for my mother, and sent me off.

The walk home was uneventful. Nobody noticed my sweatpants, nobody noticed I wasn't in class all day, and we went home via the main road. I gave Mom the bag and went to my room to sleep. I don't know if she ever looked in the bag or if she ever read the letter from the nurse-- she never asked, and I never told.

THE RULER

Most of my memories of the four-and-a-half years I spent in a Catholic elementary school are fear-based; nuns, who made up the bulk of the staff, were free to hit, slap, pinch, or squeeze in order to keep discipline. Some of them, at least it has been my lifelong belief, seemed to enjoy pushing their brand of capital punishment into sadistic pain levels.

Our principal, Sister Mary Finbarr, kept an extra wide ruler hanging from a hook in her office, and for most of the kids it was there to just intimidate, never to be used on their fragile knuckles. I guess seeing it was more than enough for these kids to get the message.

For me, and I'm guessing for some of my brothers as well, the nuns seemed to know that we needed a stronger dose of disciplinarian medicine. Besides, a ruler hanging on the principal's wall could not match Mom's emotional attacks.

The nuns did give their best effort, gaining them a high spot on my list of phobias.

One time happened towards the end of fourth grade. I was running late, as usual, and was in no mood to listen to Sister Mary Finbarr, whom I knew would be standing by her post just inside the main entrance. There was a door at each end of the building, and one out back on the loading dock, but all three could only be opened from the inside. There was also a small bump-out building on one end that I was led to believe is where the nuns lived. This had a main door in the center and a hallway that connected to the school.

There was no way in hell I would ever go in that building. My overactive imagination convinced me that if I was to ever step inside those doors, I would never be seen again. If I was lucky, decades later the authorities would find me as a toothless, bent-over old man inside a makeshift cell in the basement, living off of condensation on the mossy brick walls and eating spiders and cockroaches.

As my inexperienced brain saw it there was only one option; my homeroom was on the first floor, closer to the end of the right side of the building, and as it was a warm spring day, the windows were cracked open.

At the time I thought it was a stupid, simple plan: peek into the window, and when the teacher turned her back to write on the board, I would push the window open, hop in and be at my desk before she turned back around.

This was the beginning of my lifelong superpower of coming up with simple plans that go horribly wrong.

From the start, I should have given up and gone straight to the office, especially after I figured out the classroom was on the first floor, but the windows were still over my head. I had to keep jumping up to get a quick mid-air glimpse into the classroom. Why the teacher didn't see my melon head bobbing up and down in the window is a mystery to me: she never turned her back to me, but didn't notice me either.

I almost gave up when for some reason the teacher stepped out into the hall. I could still see her standing just outside the door frame, but her back was to me, and I grabbed it as my chance.

Looking back, I try to envision this from the angle of sitting in a car in the parking lot: a short, slightly chubby kid hanging from the sill; his legs quickly pinwheeling trying to get some traction on the brick; and almost as if he suddenly found himself on a treadmill going at top speed, his feet found traction and shot him head-first through the window.

It must have looked like a scene from *The Three Stooges*.

The story should end here with me landing on the floor and quickly getting to my seat, but there is another nasty twist to the tale.

The school was already old, built sometime in the early 50s. The school had a boiler in the basement that heated water and forced the hot water through these grill-like radiators that were in each classroom, located just under the windows. The premise was the hot water transferred the heat to the metal grill, which in turn transferred the heat into the air of the room. In the winter they worked well enough, except when in use they rattled, hissed, and banged, and would burn you if you touched the grill.

The rest of the year the teachers would cover the tops of the radiators to create extra table space. This particular year, my teacher used this space to hold the 20 or so plants the class was growing.

A few weeks prior, each of us got a paper cup filled with dirt, one tomato seed, and some colored pencils to decorate the cup any way we saw fit. The seed was planted, cups decorated, and each morning after prayers and the Pledge of Allegiance, the class would tend to the plants. The little suckers grew pretty good-

- every seed germinated-- and on the morning I catapulted myself through the window, the plants were a good four inches tall.

As I fell, more than climbed, through the window, my last sight before impact was the tomato plants were lined up like good little soldiers.

My arm hit first, sending a few cups toppling to the floor and knocking a dozen more over on the makeshift table. My torso came next, coming down hard and crushing the knocked over cups, releasing stem, roots, and dirt to splatter all over. My legs completed this delicate ballet by slamming into the table, crushing a few more cups. There was no stopping my body's momentum at that point, and it rolled to the floor, taking the makeshift table and all its plants with it.

The crash and thud were loud enough to not only bring my teacher back into the room, but two other teachers who heard it from their rooms as well.

I was still half-lying, half-sitting on the floor when the teachers rushed to the back of the room. Around me was the now split-in-half table and a dirt and Styrofoam graveyard of tomato plants.

There were no survivors.

The walk to the office was quick and painful. One of the preferred methods of torture the nuns had was to grab you by the ear and walk fast, dragging you along. It seemed they would walk at a pace they knew would be difficult for you to keep up, allowing them to pull harder on your earlobe.

By the time we reached the office, Sister Mary Finbarr was waiting, ruler in hand. The procedure was you put your hands on the desk so your knuckles were on the edge. The nuns would use a hard but quick *snap* down across the knuckles with the ruler, which sent a brief but sharp burst of pain up your arms. I always tried to fight back any tears for as long as I could, and it wasn't until I was much older that I realized once you cried, they would stop. It was like they were holding a contest.

How many whacks would it take to make you cry?

The rest of the punishment was my desk in the hallway outside the office. This was the second time my desk was banished from the classroom; the first time was in third grade when I leaned over and kissed the girl beside me on the cheek. She had snuck a note to me with two hand-drawn boxes on it. Above one was the word YES, above the other was the word NO, and the note read, "I like you, do you like me?"

Rather than mark a box, I kissed her.

There was no ruler in that incident, but I was not allowed back in the class.

THE LOCKED CLOSET

In 1976 when I was in ninth grade, my high school was considered the largest high school this side of the Mississippi. When my youngest child graduated from this same building years later, she was part of a graduating class that was close to 1000 students. Today the school houses a bank, child care center, its own police force, and a planetarium. The local saying is the high school has everything a student could want to help them succeed, all they have to do is take advantage of it.

The only issue is for all of its greatness educationally, its looks left you feeling cold and unimpressed.

I watched one of those reality shows on a maximum-security prison in the middle of the desert. They had a main building in the center with four individual cell blocks, two on each side, shooting out like square spokes on a wheel. All of the buildings were finished in a nondescript gray concrete.

The first thought I had when I saw this was, "Damn, that looks like my high school."

Not that I'm saying the school was like a prison, but it damn sure looked like the one I saw on television.

The school itself was set way back from the two main roads that intersected the property, and being surrounded by sports fields gave it that deserted look. From the road, the inset windows disappeared giving it the cold, windowless feel, and the finish was the same gray cement that would make any prison proud.

In the center of the compound was a 'pod' that held the administration offices. This was where you found the principal's office, nurse's station, and the guidance department. From there, attached by short hallways, were four other 'pods' squaring off the footprint. Each of these were identified by color; yellow and blue on one side, red and green on the other.

Now, here my creative license comes in handy because it always seemed to me each building had its own studies. If I remember it right the Yellow Building was mostly English classes; the Red Building was mostly science; Green was health; and Blue was history. Like I said, this is just what my adult self thinks my teenage self was thinking at the time.

111

This made running from building to building crazy. The hallways were so cluttered with student lockers that when the bell rang it seemed classrooms would simultaneously purge hundreds of bodies into the narrow halls as all tried to get to a locker, and to their next class, before the bell. Good luck to the poor slob that had to get from English on the third floor of the Yellow Building all the way to the other side to the second floor of the Green Building in ten minutes.

Because these buildings were self-contained-- with each having a cafeteria and library on the first floors, and classrooms and labs on the second and third floors-- I thought it would make more sense to keep students in one building for all their studies. But, who am I to say?

Completing the grounds on one side was the Fine Arts Building, which not only held woodshop and auto-mechanics, but also a full sized theatre, art studio, television studio, and a fully-functioning restaurant run by the students. On the other side was the three-story high gymnasium. This housed locker rooms that matched most professional sports arenas, an indoor Olympic-sized swimming pool, fully functioning weight room, and a gym that was large enough to hold professional boxing and wrestling matches. It's where I saw 'The Undertaker' take on all who dared enter the ring.

Even with a principal on board, each building had a Housemaster and Assistant Housemaster. To be honest I'm not sure what the Housemaster did; their office always seemed to be a flutter of activity, but what in hell all that activity was I had no clue. In my short tenure in the school, I only had one encounter with the Housemaster, and it wasn't one of my best moments.

I'll call her Mrs. C, and for her short stature, I doubt much over five feet, she had no problem exerting her authority. She had no issue randomly stopping someone in the hall and questioning where they were going, and more importantly, where they were supposed to be. It was a rare lunch that you didn't see her escorting some poor soul to the Assistant Housemaster's office.

I just found her odd. Her mousey brown hair was bowl-cut above her ears, and she always wore large, round framed glasses that seemed too big for her head. She reminded me more of an eleven-year-old nerdy boy than the second-in-command of a large city high school.

Most remember her fondly as tough but fair, and always for the students. I remember her as the odd-looking Housemaster that I locked in a closet.

It was one of those things that just happen, stupid as it was. I was heading to the buildings cafeteria for lunch, and beside the cafeteria doors was a janitor's closet that usually was closed and locked. This time not only was it wide open, but lurking just inside was Mrs. C.

The plan was quick, on the spot, and simple: with a football-like block I hit the door as I passed by, and continued on to disappear back into the crowd of students. My thoughts were Mrs. C would burst back out of the closet within moments, searching the never-ending crowd coming in and out of the cafeteria doors, but by then I would be safely inside at a table eating my American chop suey and cornbread.

What I didn't plan on was the door had an automatic lock that engaged as soon as it closed. As I unknowingly sat eating my lunch, a growing crowd of concerned and horrified students and staff were gathering around the locked door trying to calm Mrs. C. who was frantically banging to be let out. It took over 15 minutes for the janitor to get there with the key.

My name was dropped at Mrs. C.'s feet like Judas dropping his silver coins. The security officer Mr. Gentile, whose ragged nose it was rumored was bitten off by a student, called me out of my last class. Waiting out in the hallway was Mrs. C., and the two of them marched me to the Assistant Housemaster's office. Mrs. C. neither spoke nor looked at me the entire trip back to the Yellow Building.

Mr. B. was waiting for me, sitting behind his desk with his wallet on top of it. He stood, in his dark suit, looking like the enraged version of Ward Cleaver, and began an angry and loud lecture which was when I learned what really happened.

I felt bad then; I feel bad now.

From Mr. B.'s I went to Mrs. C.'s office and apologized. It was honest and heartfelt; I really did feel bad. My punishment was five days' suspension, for the rest of the year study would be spent in Mrs. C.'s office doing whatever chore she had for me, and lunch would be spent in the waiting area of Mr. B.'s office.

What about the wallet, you ask?

There was a rumor passed down by my brothers that Mr. B. had a letter from our Dad giving him permission to kick our asses if we got out of line. I personally never saw the letter. To this day, I don't know if it was really true or if Mr. B. heard about the rumor and was playing with me. Either way, whenever I was called to his office, which was more often than I care to admit, that wallet would be on his desk.

OPEN CAMPUS

Back in my day, the high school had an open campus-- basically lunch or study could be spent outside. They still frowned about openly smoking cigarettes, but didn't enforce it unless they thought you were doing something more devious.

Like smoking that devil's weed.

For that, you went to the flagpole. Outside the gymnasium was a flagpole surrounded by a waist-high stone wall that was about fourteen-foot square, and a dozen people or more could sit comfortably around it. What made it ground zero for the pot smoking crowd was the perfect vantage points. All four sides of the wall were far enough away from any door, building, or walkway to provide no ambush points. By the time anyone of importance got close, your joint was already pinched out, and you were on your way to the next class. There were also so many students there at any given time it was impossible to figure out who owned the sweet-smelling herbal cloud drifting just below the flapping red, white, and blue.

For those not as brave, there was the path.

The path was just that: a small dirt path that wound through a small patch of woods on the side of the school. It was the side that housed most of the maintenance shops, so you didn't have to worry about teachers or security guards roaming around. This was for those not fully comfortable in the open, but also some of the hardcores: the drinkers, the snorters, and those who found their motivations in little pills.

The morning before my father died, I went to the path for a private smoke, just a plain cigarette.

I went maybe thirty feet into the woods and I saw a couple of pot smokers and a kid sitting on a rock drinking from a quart-sized jug that I can only assume was filled with some high-test orange juice. None of them paid me any attention.

I had taken no more than three drags off the cigarette when someone yelled, "Cops!"

I looked down the path and the three people I saw as we came in now turned to a dozen. Kids seemed to be falling out of the trees, climbing out from under rocks, and rushing towards us in wide-eyed terror. All I had was a cigarette, but I got caught up in the mob and began running deeper into the woods, bumping into even more kids along the way.

It was a good ten minutes of blind running before I realized I was I lost. I heard yells and snapping branches in the opposite direction and almost turned to run towards them, but was too tired and already out of breath. I figured this was a city-- I was bound to come out of the woods somewhere-- and I now walked to wherever the path would take me.

The path I was on must have followed a wide loop because it ended at a small dirt hill, and when I reached the top, I was facing the back side of the skating rink, and just behind that was the Fine Arts Building of the school. The campus itself was deserted; the bell had rung.

While I was dusting dirt and leaves off my jeans, everyone else was tucked away in their homerooms. This brought on the big decision of the morning: do I go in late and come up with some lame excuse? Or do I take the long way home and call it a day?

I sat on a massive flat rock, lighting the now slightly squished half of a cigarette still in my hands, weighing my options. On one hand I haven't been in any real trouble all year. I wasn't on anybody's radar.

There was a noise. A rustling of dirt as if someone, or something, was climbing up the same side of the hill I just climbed. I stood off the rock, legs at the ready to run down the other side, when a hand came over the edge. In it was the now near-empty quart bottle of orange juice, slowly followed by the kid I saw at the entrance to the path. He was much worse the wear than I: sweat had left streaks of dirt from his forehead to his chin, and his hair which I remembered as blond was now caked with leaves, pine needles, and dirt. Even his clothes looked as if he crawled up the path instead of ran, and his slurred speech and unsteady legs suggested he might have done just that.

Today his name eludes me-- for some reason Neal comes to mind-- and I've lost to time any conversation we may have had, except he was determined to go to class. He offered me the plastic bottle and against my better judgement, I accepted. I was thirsty and took a huge gulp, the citrusy tang of the orange juice quickly turned to a burn as the vodka rushed down like shards of glass racing for my stomach. I don't remember if I gasped, choked, or gagged, but I remember "Neal" being amused, smiling at me as I handed the bottle back.

It was a tough ride down, but once the liquid settled in my belly it changed from harsh to warmth that settled over me like a blanket. I actually felt better, my mood switching from freak-out to almost calm, and I was suddenly able to decide: there would be no school for me today.

I tried talking "Neal" out of his drunken plan to still attend classes, even offered to help him clean up some, but deep within his watery, bloodshot eyes was a determination. His mind, although coated in alcohol, was on a mission. What that mission was, I'm not sure even he knew.

"Neal" slid more than climbed back down the hill, and soon came back into view, staggering across the back-parking lot. I sat there, quietly watching "Neal" until he disappeared into the Main Entrance, the bottle still in his hand. I never saw "Neal" again, and to this day have no idea what became of him, or if his mission was ever achieved.

AT JOURNEY'S END

It is only at journey's end,
With twilight slowly surrounding us,
Can we sleep a true and honest sleep.
Free from the torment of dreams,
And a lifetime of pains.
Free from the constraints of life
That binds us to a tortured soul.
Free from a carnival of emotions,
The real thief of serenity.
Now, cleansed before eternity
It is time to lay down and sleep,
A deep and freeing sleep,
And welcome a new journey
Into paradise.

JUNE 21, 2017

Mom died today.

Buddy called yesterday morning; the nursing home had sent Mom to the hospital because she was unresponsive and vomiting blood. The hospital staff suggested this would be the time to gather the family.

The brothers held vigil overnight; there were a couple of texts from Buddy, a call from my sister, messages all wanting to know if I was going to say goodbye. Everyone was either concerned, or curious, over what I was going to do, how I was going to react or if I was going to react at all.

Mom and I had made our peace already. I'm not sure anyone understands that.

Buddy called again saying it was almost time and I should come now. I drove to church instead, lit a candle, and prayed to the powers that be to ease her pain, fix her broken body and mind, and give her safe travels to a better place.

It was the most heartfelt, honest prayer I've ever made.

She died just before noon, and now it seems everyone is waiting for me to confess my sins.

Right up to the end she held court over the drama and divisions smothering the family. Based on reports of bickering and whispered judgements surrounding her hospital bed, her children once again fell prey to her need to control by any means necessary.

Even in her final weeks she continued to hold the few frayed strings that were left attached to my siblings; she told one brother another brother had a bank card of hers, and the two brothers argued and came close to physical blows. Surprisingly, neither brother questioned the motives of the woman who had a history of pitting one against the other.

It was only after the damage between the two was done that she admitted the bank card was in her bra all that time, because that card was 'none of anybody's damn business.'

Another brother faced her casual but very mean comments that finally, after 60 years, broke his heart and pushed him to the edge.

A woman who spent most of her adult life in a low-income housing project and her senior life in a low-income apartment complex was still able to convince her children to fight over money that was just not there.

If her goal was to divide and conquer what was left of our hearts and soul, then she died a happy woman. Even months after her death, three brothers are still not speaking to each other, one brother thinks the family hates him, one brother's heartbroken from the final words of a woman who was getting her last verbal punches in, and a sister is at a loss on how to fix us.

In her wake, she left behind children who are emotionally and spiritually broken.

All of us boys struggle with our own relationships; when it comes to our marriages, we have trust issues, commitment issues and cannot help but compare the actions of our significant others with the actions of our mom's, and then question their motives behind it.

Sometimes we're not so nice about that.

We also find it difficult to make and maintain friendships. We all have friends, have those we enjoy the company of, and on a casually level we are known as fun, easy going nice guys. Only we each reach a point where we push back, we find fault that wasn't there before or just walk away leaving those to wonder what the hell happen.

The worst is the struggle we have on any emotional connection with our own children. I once confessed to my wife how more often than not I would be upset over her treatment of the kids. How I felt she was too easy on them, did not discipline them enough and I felt the need to over-discipline to make up for it. It would then occur to me I had no clue how a Mom was supposed to act, and maybe I was the one that was wrong.

Maybe I was the one that didn't know how to act with my children. Maybe it was ok to just love them and be with them.

Maybe, I didn't have to be an asshole much of the time.

NOBODY SPECIAL

A broken man,
With a broken soul
Looks towards the morning horizon,
As the sun rises on a new day.
He speaks into the cool wind
Letting the words casually drift away.
I wish you peace, he whispers,
I hope you find contented rest.
But, it's time for me to move on.
It's time for me to breathe again,
Deep and free again.
It's time to stop
Being nobody special.

John Barry currently lives just south of Boston with his wife Debbie and dog Maggie. He continues to build on his relationship with his three children, Justin, Meggan and Melissa, hoping that years from now they will remember hugs.

He is currently working on his first novel of fiction, 'Where Bad Dreams Go' which he hopes to have available the summer of 2019.

Although John still considers himself an asshole, today he is able to say it with a smile.

Made in the USA
Columbia, SC
25 January 2021